Great Cases in Constitutional Law

☆

NEW FORUM BOOKS

Robert P. George, Series Editor

A list of titles

in the series appears

at the back of

the book

Great Cases in
Constitutional Law

☆

EDITED BY
ROBERT P. GEORGE

PRINCETON UNIVERSITY PRESS

PRINCETON, NEW JERSEY

Library of Congress Cataloging-in-Publication Data

George, Robert P.
Great cases in constitutional law / edited by Robert P. George.
p.   cm. — (New forum books)
Includes index.
ISBN 0-691-04951-3 (cloth : alk. paper) —
ISBN 0-691-04952-1 (pbk. : alk. paper)
1. Constitutional law—United States—Cases.   I. George, Robert P.
II. Series.
KF4549.G68 2000
342.73′02—dc21   99-045171

This book has been composed in Baskerville

The paper used in this publication
meets the minimum requirements of
ANSI/NISO Z39.48-1992 (R1997)
(*Permanence of Paper*)

http://pup.princeton.edu

Printed in the United States of America

1   3   5   7   9   10   8   6   4   2

1   3   5   7   9   10   8   6   4   2
(Pbk.)

☆ *Contents* ☆

CONTENTS

☆ *Contributors* ☆

HADLEY ARKES is Edward Ney Professor of Jurisprudence and American Institutions at Amherst College.

DONALD DRAKEMAN is President and CEO of Medarex Corporation and Lecturer in Politics at Princeton University.

JEAN BETHKE ELSHTAIN is Laura Spelman Rockefeller Professor of Social and Political Ethics at the University of Chicago.

ROBERT P. GEORGE is McCormick Professor of Jurisprudence at Princeton University.

JAMES M. MCPHERSON is George Henry Davis '86 Professor of American History at Princeton University.

EARL MALTZ is Distinguished Professor of Law at Rutgers University.

WALTER F. MURPHY is McCormick Professor of Jurisprudence Emeritus at Princeton University.

CASS R. SUNSTEIN is Karl N. Llewellyn Distinguished Service Professor of Jurisprudence at the University of Chicago.

MARK TUSHNET is Carmack Waterhouse Professor of Constitutional Law at Georgetown University Law Center.

JEREMY WALDRON is Maurice and Hilda Friedman Professor of Law at Columbia University.

GEORGE WILL, a syndicated columnist and ABC News commentator, has been a Visiting Lecturer in the Department of Government at Harvard University.

Great Cases in Constitutional Law

☆ *Introduction* ☆

ROBERT P. GEORGE

FREQUENTLY IN American history, the federal judiciary, and, particularly, the Supreme Court of the United States, has intervened
in divisive controversies involving important issues of domestic
public policy. Sometimes the form of judicial intervention has
been by way of the interpretation of laws enacted by the Congress.
The most dramatic judicial actions, however, have involved the
invalidation of acts of Congress and state legislatures by courts
deeming them to be unconstitutional. Rulings of the latter sort
are particularly significant since, according to the dominant
understanding of the scope of judicial authority under the Constitution, the invalidation of legislative acts by courts exercising
the power of constitutional "judicial review" cannot be reversed by
legislation. Only a constitutional amendment can effectively undo
such a judicial act; and, under the terms of the Constitution,
amendments are extremely difficult to achieve. Indeed, the Constitution has been formally amended only twenty-seven times in
our nation's history, and—despite the fact that in many instances
the invalidation of legislation by the courts has been unpopular—
only a small number of these amendments have had as their purpose the reversal of judicial decisions invalidating legislation as
unconstitutional.

Remarkably, the power of judicial review is nowhere expressly
granted in the constitutional text, though plainly some supporters
of the Constitution's ratification believed this power to be granted
implicitly.[1] Not long after ratification, the power was successfully
claimed by judges, who inferred its existence from the fact that
the Constitution of the United States is, by its own terms, *law*—
indeed, *the supreme law of the land*—and, as Chief Justice John
Marshall argued in his opinion for the Supreme Court in the 1803
case of *Marbury v. Madison,* "it is emphatically the province and
duty of the judicial department to say what the law is."

3

Judges exercising the power to invalidate legislation as unconstitutional commonly deny that the power they exercise is, properly speaking, political. They insist that their rulings simply give effect to the law set forth in the Constitution. They sit, after all, as judges, not as "philosopher-kings" empowered to substitute their own policy judgments for the contrary judgments embodied in law by democratically accountable legislators. From a political scientist's point of view, however, judicial review places in the hands of judges a potentially awesome form of what can only be described as political power. Interpretations of the Constitution by judges, however controversial, can effectively deprive the people and their elected representatives of the right to resolve disputed issues in accordance with the normal procedures of democratic self-government. Federal judges, as appointed rather than elected officials, are democratically *un*accountable; they serve "on good behavior"—i.e., for life unless removed by way of impeachment for serious misdeeds; and they enjoy protection against any effective form of legislative retaliation for their rulings. In light of these facts, many commentators throughout our history, including some notable judges, have called for "judicial self-restraint," lest the judiciary usurp the lawmaking authority of legislatures under the pretext of enforcing constitutional norms.

In the chapters that follow, distinguished scholars and leading commentators on American constitutional law and political theory analyze and consider the legacy of cases in which the Supreme Court of the United States, as the ultimate court of appeal in the federal system, has exercised the power of judicial review to resolve—or, at least, attempt to resolve—hotly disputed issues of public policy. In all of these cases, critics complained that the justices were, without constitutional warrant, substituting their own views about policy matters for the judgments of the people's legitimately elected representatives. In other words, critics claimed, in each case, that the decision was, in effect, an abuse of judicial power—that the Court was functioning, not as an interpreter or applier of law, but as a law*making* institution, an unconstitutional "superlegislature."

In response to these criticisms, the Court's defenders in each case argued that the decisions were fully justified as giving effect to guarantees, if merely implicit ones, of the Constitution. They maintained that the justices were right to eschew a "strict" or "narrow" reading of the Constitution in favor of a "generous" interpretation of the constitutional rights and freedoms it enshrines in our fundamental law. Where critics saw, and see, the usurpation of democratic authority by electorally unaccountable judges, defenders saw, and see, the justices functioning as guardians of constitutional ideals against the depredations of legislative majorities.

Commonly these days people think of "judicial restraint" as in principle a "conservative" cause and "judicial activism" as a "liberal" one. American history does not, however, bear out this view. Although it is true that for the past few decades the charge of "usurpation" has been leveled against the courts more frequently *just one example!* by conservatives than by liberals, it has not always been thus. Within the memory of many living Americans, the charge was hurled by supporters of Franklin Roosevelt's New Deal social and economic programs against a conservative Supreme Court that repeatedly invalidated these programs on constitutional grounds.

To focus, as we do in this volume, on the most important cases in which courts have intervened in major public policy conflicts by invalidating legislation as unconstitutional is to see that the debate over the scope of judicial review is not in principle an ideologically partisan one. Although an unprincipled approach to the subject would countenance sweeping judicial power when judges are likely to serve one's own political agenda, and condemn it when they are not, no one can securely believe that broader or narrower understandings of the scope of judicial authority will serve one's partisan interests in the long run. Today's issues may not be tomorrow's; and today's judges may well be replaced by a future cohort more, or less, likely to share one's own moral views or political faith. Prudence, then, counsels an effort to identify principled grounds for judgment about the proper scope of judicial power.

Marbury v. Madison is often cited as the case that established the power of the courts to invalidate legislation. Although some scholars believe that judicial review was exercised by the justices in one or two earlier cases, no one denies that *Marbury* effectively settled the issue of whether judicial review *of some sort* may legitimately be exercised. Unlike the later Great Cases we consider in this volume, *Marbury* did not involve a major public policy dispute going beyond the question of the scope of judicial power itself. The case concerned the rather mundane issue of the obligation of President Thomas Jefferson's secretary of state, James Madison, to deliver commissions to judges who had been appointed in the closing hours of John Adams's administration. Jefferson, of course, preferred to see the commissions remain undelivered so that Adams's "midnight appointments" would never be given effect. Marbury and other claimants argued, however, that the appointments became effective upon being signed by the president, and must therefore be delivered. The Supreme Court agreed with that proposition. However, the case turned on the procedural question of whether the congressionally enacted Judiciary Act of 1789, which Marbury cited as the source of the Supreme Court's authority to hear his case, was constitutionally valid. The justices ruled that it was not. Writing for a unanimous Court, Chief Justice Marshall held that the act unconstitutionally expanded the Court's "original jurisdiction" beyond the scope set forth in the text of the Constitution itself.

As one prominent constitutional interpretation casebook's editors observe, "Marshall's cunning handling of *Marbury v. Madison* was a masterpiece of political strategy."[2] By ruling that Congress could not expand the Supreme Court's original jurisdiction, the "Great Chief Justice" managed to invalidate a piece of federal legislation without issuing an order that Congress or the president could find any effective way of defying. In the end, Marbury's case simply faded away when he failed to pursue the matter in a lower federal court which would, unquestionably, have had original jurisdiction. And, though Jefferson famously grumbled about the Court's decision in *Marbury*, Marshall had used it to establish the formal power of the courts to invalidate legislation as unconstitutional.

Marbury left unresolved, however, the question of the scope of the power of judicial review. Alexander Hamilton had argued that the judiciary is "the least dangerous branch" of government, possessing "neither force, nor will, but merely judgment."[3] To us

6

today, these words seem quaint—even naive—in view of the entrenched power of courts to fashion public policy, for better or worse, in areas extending from abortion and affirmative action to prison conditions and public school financing. In our time, courts are, by any account, significant political actors. Judicial power has expanded far beyond what anyone imagined possible when Mr. Marbury went to court to force Mr. Madison to deliver his commission. As Mark Tushnet observes in his contribution to our volume, expansive judicial power is a substantial legacy of *Marbury v. Madison.* Yet the question *Marbury* forced onto the political agenda in 1803 is one that we Americans would continue to wrestle with throughout our national history; indeed, we continue struggling to answer it today: How much power should we entrust to electorally unaccountable judges in our constitutional democratic republic?

For several decades after *Marbury,* the Supreme Court exercised its power of judicial review sparingly. Although the Court struck down a number of state laws, it did not invalidate another significant piece of federal legislation until it intervened in the dispute over slavery in the 1857 case of *Dred Scott v. Sandford.* Scott was a slave who had been taken by Sandford, his master, into the free state of Illinois and then into free sections of the Louisiana Territory before returning with him to Missouri. Scott then brought a lawsuit claiming that his lawful residence in a free state had the legal effect of permanently freeing him from slavery. In reply, Sandford argued that Scott, as a Negro, was a citizen of neither the state of Missouri nor the United States of America; therefore he remained Sandford's property despite of his having been resident in free territory.

In a now infamous opinion by Chief Justice Roger Brooke Taney, the Supreme Court accepted Sandford's argument. By a vote of 7–2, the justices ruled that Scott was not, and could not be, a citizen. As a member of a race deemed to be "subordinate and inferior," Scott had, Taney declared, "no rights or privileges but such as those who held the power . . . might choose to grant [him]." As for his residence in free territory, the Court held that the Missouri Compromise, under the terms of which Congress

7

had admitted Missouri as a slave state but prohibited slavery in other sections of the Louisiana Territory north of thirty-six degrees, thirty minutes latitude, was unconstitutional. This denial of congressional authority to limit slavery, even in federal territories, was considered by critics of the Court to be an outrageous usurpation of congressional legislative authority; and it set the stage, in the view of many historians, for civil war.

In his First Inaugural Address, President Abraham Lincoln chastised the Court for its ruling in *Dred Scott*; and, though conceding that it binds the parties to the suit, contested the proposition that the executive and legislative branches of government must treat a decision of this nature as a rule binding on them. In the course of the Civil War, Congress enacted, and Lincoln signed, legislation inconsistent with the holding in *Dred Scott*. Then, after the war, the *Dred Scott* decision was formally undone by the ratification of the Thirteenth and Fourteenth Amendments, abolishing slavery and establishing de jure the full citizenship rights of all Americans, irrespective of race.

Cass Sunstein's contribution to our volume reflects on the *Dred Scott* decision as a cautionary tale about the wisdom of judicial interventions in large-scale sociopolitical disputes. He argues that contemporary liberals who look to courts to institute "same-sex marriage" and a "right to die," and contemporary conservatives who ask judges to strike down "racial preference policies" in hiring and promotion and the awarding of government contracts, tend to overlook or underestimate the likely negative social and political consequences of judicial efforts to settle morally charged debates about divisive issues. The majority in *Dred Scott* erred, according to Sunstein, not (or not merely) because they came down on the wrong side of the slavery issue, but because they attempted to resolve by judicial fiat an issue that, in the end, could only be resolved politically or by the force of arms. He suggests that judicial efforts to short-circuit the political process are almost certain to fail—and, in the process, to exacerbate social division and ill will. The lesson for contemporary judges confronting morally charged political issues is to seek more limited goals, and pursue them by more circumspect means—what Sunstein calls "incompletely theorized agreements."

The infamy of its decision in *Dred Scott* damaged, but did not destroy, the authority of the Supreme Court. Not long after the Union victory in the Civil War and the ratification of constitutional amendments abolishing slavery and establishing voting rights and other basic protections for the former slaves and their descendants, Congress enacted civil rights legislation to prohibit racial discrimination in public accommodations. The Supreme Court invalidated the legislation on the ground that Congress had no authority under the Constitution to enact it. Yet, despite outrage and protestation, the Court was able to make its ruling stick. Congress, in effect, acquiesced in the Court's judgment as to the limits of its constitutional power. And meaningful federal civil rights legislation was put off until the middle of the next century.

In 1905, the Supreme Court inaugurated a thirty-two-year period of what would come to be regarded as conservative "judicial activism." The so-called *Lochner* era of American constitutional jurisprudence began when the Court handed down a decision invalidating a New York state law limiting to sixty the number of hours in a week that bakery owners could "require or permit" their employees to work. Writing for a bare majority in *Lochner v. New York*, Justice Rufus Peckham declared that worker protection legislation of this sort violates the "right to freedom of contract" which, he said, was implicit in the Fourteenth Amendment's guarantee of "due process of law." The state of New York had defended its legislation as a reasonable and legitimate exercise of the traditional "police powers" of the states to protect "public health, safety, and morals." The Court, however, held that Joseph Lochner, a bakery owner who had been convicted of violating the law, was right to maintain that the law unconstitutionally deprived both him and his employees of a fundamental constitutional liberty. According to Peckham, the law advanced no genuine interest in *public* health or safety, since its purpose was not to insure, say, the purity of products offered for sale to the public by Lochner's bakery. Rather, it sought to advance a certain conception of the

9

private interests of Lochner's employees, and did so in an illegitimately paternalistic manner.

Four Justices dissented in *Lochner,* including Justice Oliver Wendell Holmes, whose dissenting opinion is considered a masterpiece of the genre. Holmes regarded the majority's allegedly implicit constitutional right to "freedom of contract" as a pure invention cooked up to rationalize the Court's usurpation of state legislative authority. As he viewed the matter, Peckham and his supporters were merely substituting their own private views regarding the morality of economic relations for the contrary views embodied in state law by the elected representatives of the people of New York. Holmes professed a certain agnosticism as to which of the competing views of economics and justice was the sounder. His point was merely that the Constitution was "not intended to embody a particular economic theory." It therefore did not matter, as far as he was concerned, whether he or other judges approved or disapproved of the theory animating New York's limitation of working hours. The matter was one for legislative, not judicial, deliberation and resolution.

During the *Lochner* era, the Supreme Court and other federal and state courts struck down hundreds of state and federal social welfare laws. Even during the Great Depression, the Supreme Court did not hesitate to strike down extremely popular New Deal programs, provoking a frustrated Franklin Roosevelt to float the idea in Congress of increasing the number of Supreme Court Justices so that he could "pack" the Court with enough new members to insure a majority for upholding his programs. That became unnecessary in 1937 when personnel changes, and, perhaps, a change of heart by Justice Owen Roberts, broke the Court's resistance to the New Deal and similar state legislative initiatives.

The *Lochner* case has become an emblem of the judicial usurpation of democratic legislative authority. To accuse judges or other constitutional interpreters of "Lochnerizing" is to criticize them for reading their own partisan views into the Constitution. Today the *Lochner* decision has few defenders. The conventional wisdom is that Holmes was right to regard the decision as a constitutionally unjustifiable—and, therefore, in its own way, unconstitutional—judicial intervention in a public policy dispute. Hadley Arkes, however, in his contribution to our volume, questions this conventional wisdom. He offers a qualified defense of Justice Peckham's method and reasoning, if not necessarily the conclusions he drew. Arkes takes Holmes and other critics of *Lochner* to task for embracing too narrow a reading of constitutional guarantees and too limited an understanding of the need for judges to look beyond the constitutional text to discern the meaning and implications of "due process" and other constitutional provisions. Although he is certainly sensitive to the need for judges to practice "self-restraint," lest they usurp legislative authority, Arkes argues that the matter, even in a case like *Lochner*, requires much more subtle and searching analysis than "positivist" critics of "judicial activism" typically imagine.

The opprobrium in which the Supreme Court came to be held as a result of its *Lochner* era jurisprudence—particularly among legal academics—was not finally eradicated until the Court struck a blow against racial injustice in the 1954 case of *Brown v. Topeka Board of Education*. In *Brown*, a formally unanimous Court (those justices who dissented in the Court's private deliberations joined with the majority to present a unified judgment to the public) ruled that racial segregation in American public schools violated the Equal Protection Clause of the Fourteenth Amendment. Segregation in schools and other public institutions had long been practiced throughout the southern states and in certain other parts of the country; though always controversial, segregation had been upheld as constitutionally permissible by the Supreme Court in the 1896 case of *Plessy v. Ferguson.* Over a powerful dissent by Justice John Harlan, who argued that ours is a "colorblind" Constitution, the Court in *Plessy* ruled that segregation in public transportation passed constitutional muster on the ground that the facilities being offered to whites and blacks respectively, though "separate," were "equal." Justice Earl Warren's opinion for the Court in *Brown*, however, declared that "separate is inherently unequal," thus effectively overturning *Plessy*. Notably, though, Warren's opinion did not endorse the "colorblind" Constitution ideal of Harlan's famous dissent. Rather, it appealed to psychological

11

Dale text
Social science evidence

and social-scientific evidence tending to show the negative effects of segregation, particularly on the self-esteem and academic performance of black youngsters.

Many commentators, both at the time of the decision and over the years since, have criticized the Court's reliance on this evidence. It is not that these commentators disagree with the decision in *Brown*—most are quick to point out that they support the essential holding of the case; it is rather that they fault the Court for not putting the decision on a firmer, more principled footing. George Kateb,[4] among others, has argued that the better stance would have been to found the opinion on the principles of the Harlan dissent in *Plessy*. However that may be, the popularity[5] of Court's decision to strike down school segregation makes it today a kind of touchstone of legitimate constitutional interpretation. In many circles, a theory of constitutional interpretation is simply disqualified if it cannot support the decision in *Brown*. Yet, Earl Maltz argues in his contribution to our volume, it is difficult—perhaps impossible—to justify *Brown* on a theory that looks to the original intent of the framers and ratifiers of constitutional provisions to discern their meaning.[6] At the same time, a decision grounded in a theory which ignores or dispenses with the "original understanding," Maltz contends, would seem to be an instance of Lochnerizing. Does the decision in *Brown*—not merely the reasoning, but the holding—for all the support it enjoys today, fail the test of post-*Lochner* era legitimacy? Maltz bites the bullet and argues that it does. *Brown* is Lochnerizing, albeit in a "good cause." But by legitimizing judicial liberation from a jurisprudence of "original understanding," the *Brown* decision leaves a legacy of expanded judicial power—a legacy, Maltz maintains, with more on the negative side of the ledger than on the positive side.

Nowhere has the dispute over constitutional interpretation and the scope of judicial power been more wrenching in our own time than in the case of *Roe v. Wade*. When, in 1973, the Supreme Court handed down its 7–2 decision invalidating long-standing state prohibitions or restrictions of abortion, the justices probably had no idea of the firestorm they would create. Is *Roe*, as its critics maintain, a simple and straightforward example of Lochnerizing? The Court in *Roe*, as the Court in *Lochner*, could point to no clear textual basis for the right they purported to be vindicating. Rather, the *Roe* majority found the right to "privacy," which, Justice Harry Blackmun insisted, was "broad enough to encompass a woman's decision to terminate a pregnancy," to be implicit in the very provision in which the *Lochner* majority had purported to find an implied right to "freedom of contract," viz., the Due Process Clause of the Fourteenth Amendment. Does *Roe*, then, represent the "second coming" of the discredited "substantive due process" doctrine of the *Lochner* era? Is it, as dissenting Justice Byron White charged, nothing more than a "raw exercise of judicial power"?

Roe's defenders insist that it is not. The apt parallel, they say, is not with *Lochner*, but with *Brown v. Board of Education*. As in the *Brown* case, *Roe* looks beyond the constitutional text and the original understanding of its specific provisions to discover a fundamental individual right that is essential to the very idea of a regime of constitutional freedom. Just as *Brown* vindicated the right to social equality of blacks and other racial minorities, *Roe* vindicates the right to personal autonomy of women. Critics of *Roe* counter, however, that the proper parallel is not with *Brown*; rather, it is with *Dred Scott*. Just as the *Dred Scott* decision deprived blacks of any legal standing or effective right to protection under law, the ruling in *Roe* robs unborn potential victims of abortion of precisely the same rights. And it deprives "we, the people," acting through the institutions of democratic self-government, of our right and responsibility to extend to unborn human beings the equal protection of the laws.

So, who is right? How are we to evaluate *Roe* and its legacy? On which side of the ledger are we to count this most controversial of modern Supreme Court decisions? In her contribution to our volume, Jean Bethke Elshtain lets us listen in as she conducts the argument with herself.

Together with the principal essays on the Great Cases and their legacies, our volume provides a commentary on each essay by a leading academician or public intellectual. The point of providing these commentaries is not to stage "debates," but to offer

13

another perspective, or focus on a different issue, or set of issues, raised by a particular case. Jeremy Waldron examines the legacy of *Marbury* from the point of view of someone deeply skeptical of the proposition that judges, rather than legislators, can most safely be trusted to resolve high matters of moral principle. James McPherson reflects on the ways in which *Dred Scott* shaped political decisions in the direction of civil war. Donald Drakeman raises questions about the "substantive" readings of the Fourteenth Amendment's Due Process Clause relied on by the Supreme Court in *Lochner* and *Roe*. Walter Murphy doubts whether "originalism," for all its intuitive appeal, can ever provide a workable interpretative approach to the sort of problem the Court confronted in *Brown v. Board of Education*. George Will argues for the importance of judging *Roe*, not on the basis of one's views about abortion but, rather, in accordance with disciplined reflection on the proper role of the judiciary in the politics of a democratic republic.[7]

These essays and commentaries are offered, not with the pretense that they provide anything approaching a comprehensive picture of the history of American constitutional law, but in the hope that readers will gain from them a richer understanding of the role played by the Supreme Court of the United States in major political conflicts at key moments of our national history. Such an appreciation, we trust, will enable citizens more fully and critically to understand what is at stake in contemporary disputes over the scope of judicial power.

These essays and commentaries are based on lectures presented by the authors in a series on Great Cases in American Constitutional Law held as part of the celebration of Princeton University's 250th anniversary. The editor is grateful to R. Douglas Arnold and Thomas Romer, who, as chairmen of Princeton's Department of Politics, offered invaluable assistance in planning the series and selecting lecturers and commentators. A debt of gratitude is also owed to Marvin Bressler, Christopher Eisgruber, Dirk Hartog, Jennifer Hochschild, Dorothy Bedford, and the Princeton University Alumni office.

NOTES

1. See Alexander Hamilton, Federalist No. 78 (May 28, 1788).

2. Walter F. Murphy, James E. Fleming, and Sotirios A. Barber (eds.), *American Constitutional Interpretation*, 2d ed. (Westbury, N.Y.: Foundation Press, 1995), 306.

3. Hamilton, Federalist No. 78, *supra*, n. 1.

4. See Kateb, "*Brown* and the Harm of Legal Segregation," in Austin Sarat (ed.), *Race, Law, and Culture: Reflections on Brown v. Board of Education* (New York: Oxford University Press, 1997), 91–109.

5. The *Brown* decision was, to be sure, not so popular among white southerners of the 1950s, many of whom joined in organized resistance to judicial desegregation orders. The decision spawned a movement, now a mere footnote to history, to impeach Chief Justice Warren.

6. For the most important recent effort to justify the result in *Brown* on originalist grounds, see Michael W. McConnell, "Originalism and the Desegregation Decisions," *University of Virginia Law Review* 81 (1995).

7. Will argues that courts have no business intervening in the public policy debate over abortion—either to invalidate anti-abortion legislation (as the Supreme Court did in *Roe*) or to require it. The matter is, he maintains, one to be resolved legislatively rather than judicially. Thus, he regards the decision in *Roe* as a classic case of judicial usurpation—not because it favored abortion (though Will himself certainly seems to oppose the broad legal permission of feticide), but because it displaced democratically enacted laws prohibiting or regulating the practice without constitutional warrant. I would direct the attention of readers who are disappointed that the present volume does not include an essay or commentary strongly favoring "abortion rights" to Ronald Dworkin's vigorous defense of *Roe* in *Life's Dominion* (New York: Alfred A. Knopf, 1993). Against the position advanced by Will (and others), Dworkin maintains that judges' moral views about abortion and its legal regulation rightly figure in their rulings which give specific content to "abstract" constitutional rights, such as the rights to free exercise of religion, due process, and equal protection. Dworkin argues that sound political morality requires something very much like the regime of legal abortion mandated by the Supreme Court; and according to his "moral reading" of the Constitution, judges and other interpreters must incorporate their conscientious judgments of the requirements of political morality

into their interpretations of the "majestic generalities" of the constitutional text. For a systematic presentation of Dworkin's general constitutional theory, see the Introduction to his volume of essays entitled *Freedom's Law: The Moral Reading of the American Constitution* (Cambridge, Mass.: Harvard University Press, 1996). For another noteworthy recent defense of the "pro-choice" and critique of the "pro-life" position, see Judith Jarvis Thomson, "Abortion," *Boston Review*, Summer 1995.

CHAPTER ONE

Marbury v. Madison
and the Theory of
Judicial Supremacy

MARK TUSHNET

NEARLY TWO CENTURIES ago the Supreme Court's decision in *Marbury v. Madison* set the nation forth on an extended experiment in political design.[1] *Marbury* articulated a theory of judicial review in which the courts could play a large role in national governance. And, though the courts did not realize *Marbury*'s full potential for many years, when they did they began to assert a theory of judicial review arguably even more potent than the one Chief Justice John Marshall developed in *Marbury*. Here I examine some contemporary understandings of *Marbury*'s theory of judicial review. I distinguish among a theory of judicial *authority*, which was all that was truly at issue in *Marbury*, and theories of judicial *exclusivity* and *supremacy*. In line with much recent scholarship—and with an argument made by former attorney general Edwin Meese III—I argue that neither *Marbury* nor any powerful account of constitutionalism supports the latter theories. Instead, ordinary citizens as well as our representatives have the authority and the responsibility to assess the constitutionality of proposed and enacted legislation. Having done so, we may shape our conduct according to our own understanding of the Constitution's requirements, even in the face of contrary Supreme Court interpretations.

We can frame the underlying issues by considering a contemporary problem. In 1982 the Supreme Court decision in *Plyler v. Doe* found unconstitutional a Texas statute denying a free public education to children of non-citizens illegally present in this country.[2]

In 1994 California's voters approved Proposition 187, an amendment to the state's constitution that, among other things, would deny a free public education to that same class of children. A federal court promptly held this part of Proposition 187 unconstitutional and barred state officials from enforcing it.[3]

Consider a series of problems with respect to Proposition 187:

1. *The legislator.* The legislature has to enact some new statutes to enforce Proposition 187. But the U.S. Constitution requires legislators to take an oath to uphold the Constitution, and California law requires them to uphold the state constitution and laws. Do those two oaths conflict? And if they do, would a legislator act in some way improperly if he or she voted to implement Proposition 187 notwithstanding the Supreme Court's decision in *Plyler?*

2. *The administrator.* After the state legislature passes implementing legislation, someone actually has to enforce Proposition 187. School administrators, for example, may have to ask about the citizenship status of the parents of children who attempt to enroll in their schools. They are supposed to refuse to admit children affected by Proposition 187. Would a school principal do something wrong if she or he followed Proposition 187 and denied admission to a child even though *Plyler* says that doing so violates the U.S. Constitution?

3. *The voter.* In deciding whether to vote for Proposition 187, each voter will have views on whether the proposal would embody a sound policy. Would a voter who thought Proposition 187 a good policy act improperly in voting for it despite *Plyler?*

The answer to these questions is, "Of course not. Legislators took an oath to support the Constitution—*the Constitution,* not the Supreme Court. What the Constitution means is not necessarily what the Supreme Court says it means. If legislators think the Court misinterpreted the Constitution, their oath allows them—indeed, it may *require* them—to disregard *Plyler.*" Similar responses are available for the administrator and the voter.

18

Explaining that answer, however, is more complicated than we might think. The first difficulty is that it seems to be in some tension with this country's strong tradition of judicial review. To understand this tradition we must look briefly back at *Marbury*. The Constitution's framers did not anticipate the major political development of the 1790s—the emergence of a national party system. The Federalist party, which controlled the government through the 1800 elections, was particularly suspicious of its opponents led by Thomas Jefferson. Party members believed that Jefferson's policies were deeply wrong, and what they saw as his commitment to a party system was inconsistent with the more basic idea that the government should be directed to achieve a nonpartisan public good. Having lost the presidential and congressional elections in 1800, the Federalists confronted what they believed was a constitutional turning point. They took advantage of the long "lame duck" period between the elections and the installation of the new administration and Congress to preserve their hold on the third branch of government. The Judiciary Act of 1801 responded to some real problems of judicial administration by creating a number of new judicial offices and by other revisions in the administration of justice. Under the circumstances, however, the Act was inevitably seen by Jefferson and his supporters as an attempt to thwart their accession to power. There was a real chance that the Jeffersonians would figure out some way to ignore the new statute.

They were given their chance by an apparent misstep by John Marshall. Congress created new judicial positions, and departing president John Adams moved to fill the posts. The appropriate documents were prepared and signed. Marshall, as secretary of state, had the responsibility of delivering these commissions to the new judges. But, apparently in the press of business, he simply overlooked his obligations to a few of the new judges. The new administration took advantage of Marshall's error to decline to deliver the commissions. William Marbury, whom Adams had named as a magistrate for the District of Columbia, filed an action in the Supreme Court seeking in order to direct James Madison, the new secretary of state, to deliver the commission. Political observers understood this lawsuit to be a Federalist challenge to the Jeffersonians' position on controlling the judiciary.

In what historians have come to regard as a political masterstroke, John Marshall, in his capacity of chief justice, managed to criticize the Jeffersonian program without forcing a direct confrontation. His opinion for the Court spent a great deal of time explaining why Madison was indeed under a legal duty to deliver Marbury's commission, and why a court could appropriately order even a high public official to do what the law required. But, Marshall said, Marbury sought his remedy from the wrong court. Not that Marbury had misread the statute book: according to the Court, the original Judiciary Act of 1789 did purport to give the Supreme Court the power to issue the remedy in just such cases. But, Marshall continued, that provision in the 1789 act was unconstitutional, and the courts therefore could not do what it directed them to do.

Observers both then and later found much to criticize in Marshall's opinion: his reading of the 1789 Judiciary Act, his analysis of Marbury's entitlement to a remedy, the constitutional interpretation that led him to find the 1789 act's provision unconstitutional. But the assertion that the courts had the *power* of judicial review was hardly noteworthy. The Constitution's framers assumed that the new national courts would have the power to hold statutes unconstitutional, because, as they saw it, such a power was inherent in the very idea that a written constitution adopted by the people was superior to any statutes adopted by the people's representatives. Over the previous decades, both state courts and the national courts had assumed that they did have the power to hold statues unconstitutional, and a few state courts had actually done so.

But, if *Marbury*'s assertion of the power of judicial review was not novel, some of Marshall's words opened the way to a broader view of the courts' power. In particular, in defending judicial review, Marshall wrote, "It is emphatically the province and duty of the judicial department to say what the law is." This can be read in at least two ways. Marshall might have been saying, "Look, if you pass a statute asking us to do something—in *Marbury*, hear a particular class of cases—you can't keep us from saying what the law is. And the Constitution itself says that it is law—indeed, supreme law." On this reading, Marshall's statement simply refers to what *courts do*. It has nothing to say about the constitutional duties and powers of other departments, state officials, and ordinary citizens.

The second reading, however, does treat the courts and not just the Constitution as supreme: "It is emphatically the province and duty of *the judicial department*—and no one else—to say what the law is. Once we say what the law is, that's the end of it. After that, no one obliged to support the Constitution can fairly assert that the Constitution means something different from what we said it meant."

Recently the Supreme Court, without dissent on this point, seems to have adopted this broader reading. In 1990 the Supreme Court held that the First Amendment's Free Exercise Clause invalidated only statutes that were intentionally designed to burden religious practices, and did not make "neutral laws of general applicability" unconstitutional.[4] This decision was immediately controversial, and an unprecedentedly broad coalition of interest groups—encompassing the American Civil Liberties Union and the Christian Coalition—mobilized to get around it. Congress responded by enacting the Religious Freedom Restoration Act. Purporting to exercise its power under Section 5 of the Fourteenth Amendment, which gives Congress the power "to enforce, by appropriate legislation," the Amendment's provisions, Congress prohibited any government from substantially burdening the free exercise of religion even by a neutral law of general applicability unless the burden promoted a compelling governmental interest and was the least restrictive means of doing so.

The city of Boerne, Texas, a suburb of San Antonio, believed that it could revitalize the town by creating a historic preservation district to attract tourists. St. Peter Catholic Church was in the district. The number of parishioners at St. Peter's had grown to the point where the old building could not accommodate the new population. St. Peter therefore sought permission to enlarge its building. The city refused the permit, and St. Peter sued, asserting that the city's actions violated its rights under the Religious Freedom Restoration Act. The Supreme Court eventually held the act unconstitutional. Section 5, Justice Anthony Kennedy argued for the Court, gave Congress only the power to *remedy* violations of other provisions in the Fourteenth Amendment. But Congress cannot remedy things that are not unconstitutional. Because the Court had declared that neutral laws of general applicability were not unconstitutional, there was nothing for Congress to remedy: "When the Court has interpreted the Constitution, it has acted within the province of the Judicial Branch, which embraces the duty to say what the law is. When the political branches of the Government act against the background of a judicial interpretation of the Constitution already issued, it must be understood that in later cases and controversies the Court will treat its precedents with the respect due them under settled principles, including *stare decisis,* and contrary expectations must be disappointed."[5]

Much in Justice Kennedy's statement here turns out to be clearly correct, particularly, as we will see, his point that people should expect the courts to adhere to settled precedents in later cases. But the rhetoric of judicial supremacy suggests a broader and more problematic understanding of the proper relations among the Constitution, the courts, and everyone else.

Two Episodes of Judicial Supremacy

Why would anyone think that judicial supremacy was the right way to understand our Constitution? It would not be surprising to find judges supporting judicial supremacy; it makes their job more important and interesting. But there is more to the position than self-interest.

In 1958 the Supreme Court faced a challenge to its authority in the Little Rock, Arkansas, school desegregation case of *Cooper v. Aaron.*[6] Four years earlier, *Brown v. Board of Education* had held school segregation to be unconstitutional. The Court then held that states had to desegregate their schools "with all deliberate speed." Responding to a lawsuit and orders from lower federal

courts, the school board in Little Rock developed a plan to desegregate the city's schools gradually. The state's governor, Orval
Faubus, opposed desegregation and generated a large public controversy over Little Rock's plan. As the school board put it in its
brief to the Supreme Court, the "legislative, executive, and judicial departments of the state government opposed . . . desegregation . . . by enacting laws, calling out troops, making statements
vilifying federal law and federal courts, and failing to utilize state
law enforcement agencies and judicial processes to maintain public peace."

The lower federal courts found that the public disorder was a
reason to delay desegregation. The Supreme Court disagreed.
More important here, it rejected Governor Faubus's claim that he
was not required to follow *Brown*'s directives. Relying on Marshall's statement, the Court asserted that *Marbury* "declared the
basic principle that the federal judiciary is supreme in the exposition of the law of the Constitution." Calling that principle "a permanent and indispensable feature of our constitutional system,"
the Court said that "it follows that the interpretation of [the Con-
stitution] enunciated by this Court in the *Brown* case is the supreme law of the land." The oath to support the Constitution that
Governor Faubus and state legislators took gave that interpretation "binding effect."

The Little Rock case presented a particularly appealing setting
for asserting judicial supremacy. *Brown* was unquestionably right,
or so the justices and a large part of the country thought. Governor Faubus's resistance had provoked a real crisis of law and
order, with white opponents of desegregation credibly threaten-
ing to inflict violence on anyone—including African American
children—who tried to desegregate the schools. And the Court
correctly asserted that a century and a half of judicial review had
led many Americans to believe that the Court's constitutional interpretations were indeed supreme.

But there are other cases where strong assertions of judicial supremacy are less appealing. The notorious *Dred Scott* case makes
the point.[7] The case arose when Dred Scott, held as a slave in
1836, was taken by his owner to the free territory of Minnesota for

several years. After Scott and his owner returned to Missouri, a slave state, Scott sued for his freedom, claiming that he had become free because of his residence in Minnesota. Hoping to take contention over slavery off the national political agenda in the 1850s, the Supreme Court held congressional efforts to restrict the expansion of slavery into the nation's territories unconstitutional. According to the Court, Congress lacked affirmative power to do so, and denying slave owners the right to take their slaves into the territories deprived the slave owners of their property without due process of law.

After the Court's decision, Abraham Lincoln offered an alternative to judicial supremacy. Debating Democrat Stephen Douglas during their 1858 campaign for the Senate, Lincoln replied to Douglas's effort to defuse the slavery controversy by relying on the Court's decision. Douglas said that the courts were created "so that when you cannot agree among yourselves on a disputed point you appeal to the judicial tribunal which steps in and decides for you, and that decision is binding on every good citizen." Using language not that much different from the Court's in *Cooper v. Aaron*, Douglas said that when the courts resolved the questions, that was the end of it: "When such decisions have been made, they become the law of the land."[8]

Lincoln would have none of it. He agreed that the Court's decision resolved the precise controversy before it; Dred Scott would remain a slave. But he rejected the decision "as a political rule which shall be binding on the voter . . . [or] binding on the members of Congress or the President to favor no measure that does not actually concur with the principles of that decision."[9]

In his First Inaugural Address, delivered even as the South prepared for war over slavery, Lincoln again made his position clear. *Dred Scott* was "binding . . . upon the parties." In addition, the Court's decisions were "entitled to a very high respect and consideration in all parallel cases by all other departments." Even an "erroneous" decision could be followed when "the evil effect of following it, being limited to that particular case, with the chance that it may be overruled and never become a precedent for other

24

cases, can better be borne than could the evils of a different practice." But, Lincoln continued, "the people will have ceased to be their own rulers" if "the policy of the government, upon vital questions affecting the whole people, is to be irrevocably fixed by decisions of the Supreme Court, the instant they are made, in ordinary litigation between parties in personal actions."[10]

Lincoln was a subtle constitutionalist, and his statements contain nearly everything we need to work out a theory that would explain the result in *Cooper v. Aaron* without committing us to a strong theory of judicial supremacy.[11]

COMPLEXITIES IN SOME SEEMINGLY EASY CASES:
PARDONS AND VETOES

We can begin by noting a peculiar feature of *Cooper v. Aaron*. There was no judicial order directing Governor Faubus himself to desegregate the Little Rock schools. So, in the narrowest sense, Faubus's position was entirely consistent with Lincoln's: at least in a purely legal sense, Governor Faubus was not refusing to comply with a judicial order in a case already resolved against him.

Of course everyone knew that Governor Faubus *could be* brought into a lawsuit. If he continued his resistance after that, he would directly present the question of judicial supremacy. In Justice Anthony Kennedy's terms, he could expect the Court to adhere to *Brown* "in later cases and controversies" arising directly out of the Little Rock school crisis. But it is worth pausing to think about situations in which it might seem that an official could reject the Supreme Court's constitutional interpretations without running the risk of becoming the defendant in a lawsuit—situations in which no later case or controversy is likely to arise.

The classic examples involve Presidents Thomas Jefferson and Andrew Jackson.[12] As political controversy intensified in the 1790s, Jefferson's opponents controlled Congress and the presidency. They enacted a law making it a crime to criticize the president (but not the vice president, who happened to be Jefferson).

Several of Jefferson's political allies were convicted under this antisedition statute. Jefferson pardoned them after he took office in 1801, asserting that the statute violated the First Amendment's protection of free speech.

A few years later Jefferson explained his position to Abigail Adams, the wife of his Federalist adversary John Adams.[13] "You think it devolved on the judges to decide on the validity of the sedition law. But nothing in the Constitution has given them a right to decide for the Executive, any more than to the Executive to decide for them. . . . The judges, believing the law constitutional, had a right to pass a sentence . . . because that power was placed in their hands by the Constitution. But the Executive, believing the law to be unconstitutional, was bound to remit the execution of it; because that power has been confided to him by the Constitution." If the judges could "decide what laws are constitutional . . . for the Legislature and Executive also, [this] would make the judiciary a despotic branch." As Jefferson saw it, his constitutional power to pardon authorized him—indeed, he said, *required* him—to act on his judgment that the antisedition law was unconstitutional even though the courts had upheld it.[14]

Andrew Jackson had a similar view. In 1819 the Supreme Court held that the Constitution gave Congress the power to create a national bank. Jackson disagreed with that decision. When his political opponents tried to make renewing the bank's charter a political issue, Jackson happily vetoed the proposal. He told Congress that the "opinion of the judges has no more authority over Congress than the opinion of Congress has over the judges, and on that point the President is independent of both."[15]

These cases differ from our *Plyler* problem in several ways. There is no obvious way to get judicial review of a veto or a pardon even if the president's decision is made entirely on constitutional grounds. In addition, we might think that presidents can veto laws and pardon people for policy as well as constitutional reasons. Even if we somehow devised ways of reviewing vetoes and pardons, we would not be able to distinguish between decisions based on the president's constitutional interpretations and those based

26

on merely policy grounds. Jackson's veto of the bank recharter, for example, prefaced its constitutional argument with several arguments that the bank was a bad idea because, among other things, it gave too much power to its private owners. And finally, Jefferson and Jackson acted on their views that certain laws were *unconstitutional* in the face of judicial determinations that the laws were constitutionally permissible. In contrast, the *Plyler* problem involves an official who believes that a statute is constitutional in the face of a decision that it is not.

These differences, while real, may not be important in developing an argument against judicial supremacy. Students of the U S Constitution are comfortable with the idea that some decisions, even constitutional decisions, may not be subject to judicial review. The Supreme Court itself has devised an important rule, the political question doctrine, that leaves some constitutional decisions to Congress and the president with no possibility of judicial review.

Such a rule, however, is not an inherent part of a constitutional system.[16] We could design ways of ensuring that presidential decisions to pardon or veto on constitutional grounds could be reviewed by the courts. For example, we could interpret the Constitution to require the president to veto bills *only* on constitutional grounds, or *only* on policy grounds. In the first situation, if the president's veto message asserted either a policy ground or a constitutional interpretation that the Court rejected, the courts could invalidate the veto and the bill would become law. In the second, a veto message asserting a constitutional ground, as Jackson's did, would be ineffective even if it contained policy arguments against the bill as well.[17]

Odd as this system sounds to contemporary U.S. ears, the proposition that the president's veto power was limited had some support in the nation's early years. According to one study, from 1789 to 1840 presidents vetoed twenty-one bills, "and only five or six were based upon other than constitutional grounds."[18] We might take this practice to indicate an understanding that bills ought to be vetoed only on constitutional grounds as a general rule, albeit with some exceptions. But, whether or not there was such an understanding, it surely is possible to design a system in which the president's veto power is limited. And in such a system, judicial review would always be possible.[19]

Some decisions are not open to judicial review under the present U.S. constitutional system. But that does not in itself fatally undermine the theory of judicial supremacy. The limits on judicial review show at most that, as we understand our system today, the domain of judicial supremacy might not be as extensive as we can imagine it to be. As law professor Michael Stokes Paulsen puts it, "If it is illegitimate for the President to defy 'the law' (as declared by the courts) where his actions *can* be reviewed, it is no less illegitimate for the President to defy the law where his actions *cannot* be reviewed."[20] And conversely, if it is legitimate to defy the courts when an official's actions *cannot* be reviewed, it is legitimate to do so when they *can*.

With this in the background, the difference between officials like Presidents Jefferson and Jackson, who reject a prior judicial determination that a statute is constitutional, and those like Governor Faubus, who reject a determination that a statute is *un*constitutional, dissolves. The courts said to the presidents, "You can do this if you think it appropriate on policy grounds, but you don't have to." Now supplement their statement: "You can do this if you think it appropriate on policy grounds, and you *must* do it if your only objections are constitutional, because *we* think it is constitutional." An official who refuses to act on constitutional grounds—who vetoes a bill rather than signs it, who refuses to prosecute for violating the antisedition act—is defying the courts just as much as a person who acts pursuant to a statute the courts have held unconstitutional.[21]

In short, the fact that our constitutional system does not have a way to get the courts to review some official decisions that conflict with the courts' constitutional interpretations does not really counter the theory of judicial supremacy. It identifies an awkward procedural "defect" in our constitutional system without rejecting the theory directly.

IGNORING THE COURTS

When may a legislator disregard the courts' constitutional interpretations? As Lincoln's analysis indicates, sometimes legislative action that is apparently inconsistent with a prior judicial constitutional interpretation is not inconsistent with a general theory of judicial supremacy. As his analysis also indicates, sometimes it is. But in *those* situations the case for judicial supremacy is weak and the case for a certain kind of populist constitutional law is strong.

Start with the first set of situations, where a legislator's apparent rejection of a court's constitutional interpretation actually is not inconsistent with judicial supremacy.

- A legislator could certainly support proposals that "actually concur[red] with the principles" the courts laid down. Supporting a proposal does not challenge judicial supremacy if the proposal is different from the one the courts held unconstitutional. Of course the legislator cannot know whether the courts will actually distinguish the proposal. For example, after *Dred Scott*, an abolitionist senator might have wanted to exercise Congress's power to "exercise exclusive Legislation" over the seat of government by abolishing slavery in the District of Columbia. That power is different from the power to "make all needful Rules and Regulations respecting" the territories, at issue in *Dred Scott*. A lawyer could credibly argue that an "exclusive" power is broader than a power to make "needful" rules, and therefore that the District of Columbia proposal did not conflict with *Dred Scott*. What about *Dred Scott*'s due process holding? Perhaps a lawyer could treat that as a legal analysis unnecessary to dispose of *Dred Scott* and therefore not controlling in later cases. The Supreme Court might not agree with either of these efforts to distinguish *Dred Scott*. Enacting the District of Columbia statute does not reject the Court's constitutional interpretation even so, if the legislator can make a legally credible argument that the cases are different.

Governor Faubus, however, could not make a legally credible argument that the situation in Little Rock was distinguishable from the situation anywhere else affected by the Court's desegregation decisions. There was public tension in many places, for example, and white opposition to desegregation was no more intense in Little Rock than it was in southern Virginia or South Carolina, where two of the Court's desegregation cases arose.

Finally, what of Proposition 187? It contains a provision barring aliens not lawfully present in the country from receiving publicly funded nonemergency medical services. That provision is clearly distinguishable—in the appropriate sense—from the one held unconstitutional in *Plyler*. There the Court thought it important to its constitutional analysis that the children denied a free public education were likely to remain in the country for many years, and would be more productive contributors to the nation if they had an education. Nonemergency medical services might be different, because they might be more easily available from private charitable sources, and because the social consequences of denying them might be less substantial. Of course, a court might disagree and find nonemergency medical services indistinguishable from education.[22] But the legal argument that the cases are different has enough credibility to make legislative support of *this* provision of Proposition 187 consistent with judicial supremacy.

What about the denial of a free public education? In *Plyler* the Court found no indication in the record that the burdens the children placed on the Texas economy were significant, and suggested that the outcome might differ if there had been such evidence. Proponents of Proposition 187 may reasonably hope to place appropriate evidence of such burdens in the record. The *Plyler* opinion itself indicates that this might be enough to distinguish the cases.

• A legislator need not take the controlling precedent as a "political rule," according to Lincoln. Lincoln meant that legislators could support laws that were distinguishable from the one the Court held unconstitutional, but we can give the term a somewhat broader meaning.

Sometimes the Court's doctrine makes what legislatures have actually done relevant to its constitutional interpretations. The Court's death penalty cases, for example, make "evolving stan-

dards of decency" the benchmark for deciding whether a prac
tice violates the Eighth Amendment's ban on "cruel and unusual
punishments." The Court looks to the statutes enacted by state
legislatures in determining what those standards are. In holding
unconstitutional the imposition of capital punishment for what
it described as a simple rape, the Court emphasized that only a
single state's legislature authorized the death penalty in such
cases.[23] In contrast, when it refused to find it unconstitutional to
execute people who were sixteen or seventeen when they murdered their victims, the Court found that many of the states with
capital punishment allowed the execution of those who murdered
as youths.[24]

The Court in *Plyler* took Congress's inaction into account in
finding that there was no national policy that supported denying
education to the affected children. The Court stressed that Congress had primary responsibility over immigration and naturaliza-
tion, and that Congress had done nothing to indicate its belief
that those children should be denied a free public education.
Congress has considered amending the immigration laws to authorize states to deny free public education to such children. In
light of the Court's analysis in *Plyler*, there is certainly no impropri-
ety when a senator supports such an amendment: The "principle"
of *Plyler* is not obviously inconsistent with a national law restricting
education in that way.

But when Proposition 187 was adopted, and even through
1997, Congress had not enacted such a law, and for many of the
reasons the Court itself gave: Congress was apparently still trou-
bled by the social consequences of denying free public education.
So, although parts of Proposition 187 are readily distinguishable
from *Plyler*, the one dealing with education is not.

A change in national policy—perhaps even one not expressly
about education for those children—would be relevant to assess-
ing the constitutionality of Proposition 187. Again, when Proposition 187 was adopted and through 1997, there had not been such
a change in national policy, so a legislator could not rely on this
interpretation of the "political rule" exception to justify supporting Proposition 187.

- A legislator might disregard an apparently controlling precedent, Lincoln suggested, when it was reached in "ordinary litigation between parties in personal actions." Lincoln's meaning here is not entirely clear because he does not spell out the distinction he has in mind between "ordinary litigation" and "extraordinary litigation." We can make sense of the distinction, however. The problem with a precedent set out in ordinary litigation is that the litigation may not have attracted enough public attention for the courts to have been fully informed of the case's significance. At the most basic level, the lawyers for the losing party may not have been very good even though there were many extremely good lawyers who would have leaped at the chance to represent that side—had they known the case was pending.

Even *Dred Scott* was not "ordinary litigation" in this sense. Every politically alert lawyer knew that the case was important, and the lawyers who represented Scott in the Supreme Court were among the nation's most distinguished. The same could be said about *Brown v. Board of Education* and *Plyler*. Neither Governor Faubus nor a California legislator could reasonably dismiss the applicable precedents on the ground that they had been rendered in ordinary litigation.

- According to Lincoln, a legislator may support a law indistinguishable from one held unconstitutional when there is a "chance that [the earlier decision] might be overruled." Here Justice Kennedy's reference to expectations that include the principle of *stare decisis* is obviously relevant as well. The easiest way to give the Court a chance to overrule a precedent is to enact a statute indistinguishable from the one it held unconstitutional.[25]

For example, in 1996 a federal court of appeals held unconstitutional a Texas university affirmative action policy. The policy set up two admission tracks to the state's main public law school. By the time the appeals court decided the case, the law school had changed its policy, but the new one still took race into account in weighing applicants' credentials. The court of appeals held the original policy unconstitutional because, it said, the Constitution barred states from taking race into account in any way in admissions. The Supreme Court refused to hear the law school's appeal.

Two justices noted that the case was not a good one to consider the court of appeals' broad constitutional holding because everyone agreed that the old policy used to deny the plaintiffs' applications was unconstitutional.[26]

The court of appeals decision applies to public law schools in Texas, Louisiana, and Mississippi. Can the dean of Mississippi's law school direct its admissions committee to continue to take race into account? In some sense, that directive would amount to defiance of the court of appeals' legal ruling. But it seems unduly harsh to chastise the dean for defying the courts when the obvious purpose behind the directive is to set up a new test case, one that the Supreme Court *would* find suitable for review.[27]

What evidence does a legislator need to have to think there is such a chance? Sometimes the Court itself indicates its discomfort *dissents* with its precedent. Strong dissents may show that the justices find the scope of the precedent troublesome. Or the Court may limit *limiting* the precedent, distinguishing it in new cases in ways that are le- *the* gally credible but not terribly persuasive. The fact that the justices *precedent* find it necessary to limit the reach of a precedent may suggest that they would overrule it, given the chance.

There is another way for the Court to show there is a "chance" that a decision will be overruled. In 1940 the Supreme Court upheld a state law requiring all students to salute the national flag, even if they had religious objections to doing so, as Jehovah's Witnesses did.[28] There was only one dissent. Following a spate of terrorism directed at Jehovah's Witnesses, four justices indicated in a case involving a different legal issue raised by Jehovah's Witnesses that they now thought the 1940 decision was wrong. By counting heads, lawyers could see that the 1940 decision was ripe for overruling. A lower court held a flag salute statute unconstitutional even though it was indistinguishable from the one upheld in 1940. The Supreme Court promptly affirmed the lower court's decision and overruled the 1940 precedent.[29]

Some lawyers express discomfort at this sort of head counting.[30] We are, it is said, a government of laws and not of men and women. Counting heads to see what the Court will say the Constitution means makes it dramatically apparent that at least to

counting heads[33]

some degree we are indeed a government of men and women. Whatever the theoretical merits of that concern, I doubt that a legislator is somehow required to ignore what he or she knows to be a fact, that the Court's composition affects its constitutional rulings.

Again, however, Governor Faubus could not reasonably think in 1957 that the Supreme Court was likely to repudiate its desegregation decisions, handed down only a few years earlier. There had indeed been some changes in the Court's composition, but the new appointees were likely to support the desegregation decisions. In fact, when the Court announced *Cooper v. Aaron*, it took an unprecedented course: the Court's opinion was announced under the name not of the Court or of any individual justice, but under the names of them all. And the opinion expressly said, "Since the first [desegregation decision] three new Justices have come to the Court. They are at one with the Justices still on the Court who participated in that basic decision as to its correctness." Governor Faubus should have known that from the beginning.

The *Plyler* case, however, is quite different. The Court's composition has changed dramatically since *Plyler*. Only one justice in the Court's liberal majority remained on the Court when Proposition 187 was adopted, whereas Justices William Rehnquist and Sandra Day O'Connor, who dissented in *Plyler*, have been joined by two other justices, Antonin Scalia and Clarence Thomas, whose constitutional theories make it clear that they would vote to overrule *Plyler*. That head count makes four, so a legislator could not be as sure about overruling as in the flag salute cases. And there is an additional complication. In reaffirming what they called the "core holding" of the Court's 1973 abortion decision, three justices—O'Connor, Kennedy, and David Souter—coauthored a joint opinion that stressed the importance of stability in constitutional law and said that, although they might not agree with the basic abortion decisions, they would not overrule them.[31] A legislator therefore could not confidently count even Justice O'Connor among those likely to vote to overrule *Plyler*.

But, as we have seen, the legislator does not need a guarantee. All the legislator needs is some reasonable ground for believing that the Court would overrule *Plyler* if given the chance. The head count is enough to make it constitutionally responsible for a legislator to support Proposition 187 on the ground that there is sufficient chance that the Court would overrule *Plyler*.

CONSTITUTIONAL CRISES AND THE
RULE OF LAW

We have now "solved" the *Plyler* problem with which we began, but we have done so in a way fully compatible with a general theory of judicial supremacy. To make further progress, we have to confine our attention to Governor Faubus.

• Lincoln thought there were some "evils" associated with disregarding clearly controlling Supreme Court precedents. To understand what those evils are, consider first a different case. In 1989 and again in 1990 the Supreme Court held unconstitutional state and national laws making it a crime to burn flags in political protests.[32] A clear majority of the nation's people continue to think that those decisions were deeply wrong.[33] Suppose a prosecutor discovers an anti-flag-burning statute that has not yet been held unconstitutional by her or his state's courts, and decides to prosecute a political protestor for burning a flag. The prosecutor accomplishes relatively little other than making political points by bringing the criminal case: a court is sure to dismiss the prosecution because the statute violates the Constitution, and the prosecutor will have imposed on the defendant some costs in money, time spent on the defense, and emotional distress.[34]

Now consider what Governor Faubus might reasonably have thought he could accomplish by his actions, and again put aside the obvious observation that he thought he would win political points among Arkansas's whites by the stance he took. Here too the answer is, "Not much." His actions were highly likely to generate and exacerbate social tensions, as they did. Any injunctions courts issued directing him to stop would be much less likely to repair the disruption than dismissing a frivolous prosecution would.

There is another "evil" associated with disregarding Supreme Court precedents. Doing so is inconsistent with a powerful national tradition of deference to the Supreme Court, a tradition that in its strongest version takes the form of a general theory of judicial supremacy. That theory might be wrong, but it certainly is relevant to someone deciding whether to disregard a controlling precedent. As Governor Faubus's actions did, disregarding precedents may provoke a constitutional crisis as the public sees a legislator or executive official "defying" the Supreme Court.

• But there is nothing wrong in principle with constitutional crises as such. Or, to adapt Lincoln's phrase, a constitutional crisis may be a good thing when "vital questions affecting the whole people" are involved. Senator Daniel Patrick Moynihan suggested a variation on this approach.[35] He thought that Congress could pass a law inconsistent with a Supreme Court decision to signal the Court of the deep disagreement its decision provoked.

It will be helpful to develop a distinction between two forms a constitutional crisis can take, although in the end the two forms turn out to be identical. Take the flag-burning prosecution first. A court dismissing the prosecution, it would seem, need not be relying on a general theory of judicial supremacy. As in the limited reading of *Marbury*, a judge dismissing the prosecution could say, "Look, when you bring a criminal prosecution you are asking *me* to do something. And when you do that, you have to live with the fact that among the things I do is interpret the Constitution. You can't get me to go along with you unless I agree with you about what the Constitution means. And I don't."

Governor Faubus seems to be in a different position. He was not asking the courts to do anything. *Cooper v. Aaron* thus seems to raise the question of judicial supremacy in a way that the flag-burning prosecution does not. If the courts issued an injunction against Governor Faubus, his disregard of their constitutional interpretations would be open defiance in a way that the prosecutor's filing charges is not.

But it really is not different. After the injunction is issued, Governor Faubus might say, "I don't care what you say, I'm going to continue to oppose desegregation. Put me in jail for contempt of court if you have the troops to do so." After the flag-burning prosecution is dismissed, the prosecutor might say, "I don't care what you say. I've sent the police to throw the protestor in jail. Send troops to get her out."

Once again, Abraham Lincoln provides our best example. Shortly after his inauguration Lincoln faced serious military opposition in Maryland. He directed his military commander to arrest suspected secessionists and imprison them in military jails. The commander arrested John Merryman, a lieutenant in a secessionist unit that had burned some bridges to obstruct the movement of troops and supplies. Merryman's lawyers asked Supreme Court chief justice Roger Taney, who had written the leading opinion in *Dred Scott*, for a writ of habeas corpus to release Merryman. Taney issued the writ, which directed the military commander to bring Merryman to court. But Lincoln had issued his own order suspending the writ, so the commander refused. Taney then stated that Lincoln's suspension was unconstitutional and directed Merryman's release. Taney knew, however, that his orders were futile. "I have exercised all the power which the constitution and laws confer upon me, but that power has been resisted by a force too strong for me to overcome."[36] Lincoln's position in *Merryman* shows that even the apparently modest interpretation of *Marbury* ultimately raises questions of judicial supremacy: everything a legislator or executive official can try to do using the courts, he or she can also do without using them.

Yet, as we have seen, it really does look like we have a constitutional crisis when a public official does those things. Are there any criteria for identifying when a constitutional crisis is a good thing? Here it will help to tone down the rhetoric a bit. Conflicts between the courts and the president or Congress have two dimensions. They implicate the substance of the constitutional provision at issue, and they also implicate the general question of judicial supremacy. Conflicts provoke one type of constitutional crisis when the constitutional provision is a "big" or important one like habeas corpus or the First Amendment. They provoke a different kind when the substantive provision is a smaller or more technical one.

37

Lincoln's formulation—when the "vital interests of the people as a whole" are affected—points in the right direction. Who is going to specify what those interests are? Certainly people will disagree about what they are, and we would not have a good constitutional system if anyone who wanted to reject a court's interpretation of the Constitution could get up and say, "Well, this is a vital interest of the people as a whole, so it's time for a constitutional crisis."

Instead, only those who speak for "the people as a whole" can fairly identify their vital interests. It would have to be a political leader.

But not just any political leader, either. In the face of disagreement over what the people's vital interests are, a political leader will have to forge substantial agreement on the proposition that the position he or she is asserting really does involve those interests. When an important constitutional provision is involved, we will face the "evils" of a constitutional crisis that cannot be resolved except at high cost, a cost we ought to bear in extraordinary situations but not routinely. Political leaders may provoke a major constitutional crisis and attempt to persuade the public that their view should prevail, when they are faced with an issue crucial to their political program. We have rarely faced these problems precisely because political leaders have regularly calculated that they ought not provoke a crisis either because the issue was not of such great importance or because they believed they could not prevail in a crisis.

The political leader's task differs when the constitutional provision is a less important or merely technical one. At this point we should bring into the discussion the most recent prominent opponent of a general theory of judicial supremacy—Reagan administration attorney general Edwin Meese III. Meese made a widely noted and highly criticized speech in 1986, asserting that Supreme Court decisions "do not establish a 'Supreme Law of the Land' that is binding on all persons and parts of government, henceforth and forevermore."[37] Although this sounds a lot like Lincoln, whom Meese explicitly invoked, liberals who admire Lincoln nonetheless found Meese's position a threat to the constitutional order. Why did people think that Meese's position raised the specter of a constitutional crisis, but do not see such a crisis looming when the courts disregard congressional and executive interpretations *they* think wrong—that is, when the courts exercise the power of judicial review?

Meese did not articulate his position with anything like the subtlety Lincoln had. And he was asserting it on behalf of an administration that sought to reject judicial supremacy primarily with respect to the presidency's prerogatives. Those prerogatives are important in our constitutional system, but neither Meese nor President Reagan proved able to make the case to the public that a vital interest of the people was affected when the courts directed executive officials to follow judicial interpretations of the Constitution and federal statutes.

The problems Meese and President Reagan faced were serious ones, in their eyes. But the public did not initially—or, as it turned out, eventually—think that they were great enough to justify acting against our tradition of judicial supremacy. President Reagan should have understood that his difficulty arose from public willingness to accept a general theory of judicial supremacy. Leadership in those circumstances meant attempting to undermine that public belief gradually, by selecting a highly technical issue on which to "defy" the courts and then persuading the public that the courts' constitutional interpretations come at too high a cost to public policy. If political leaders succeed once, they will have reduced public belief in judicial supremacy, and may be able to make a bolder move next time.

The basic idea here is that a constitutional crisis or efforts to bring about a gradual transformation in public views about judicial supremacy may be acceptable when able political leaders lead the public to understand that the people's vital interests are at stake. Success matters because failure imposes costs of disruption without accomplishing anything. Of course, success and failure come in degrees, and sometimes a partial success will be enough to justify the associated costs. But actions in conflict with our tradition of judicial supremacy have to accomplish *something* to offset the "evils" associated with such actions. Governor Faubus was

39

unable to persuade the people of the United States that their vital interests were at stake in Little Rock, and neither was President Reagan able to do so in the 1980s, despite the latter's manifest ability as a communicator of core ideas to the public.

And, strikingly, neither was Lincoln. He understood that slavery was one of those extraordinary cases in which the nation had to accept extraordinary costs to resolve a constitutional crisis. As he put it in a chilling passage in his Second Inaugural Address, "Yet, if God wills that [the war] continue until all the wealth piled by the bond-man's two hundred and fifty years of unrequited toil shall be sunk, and until every drop of blood drawn with the lash shall be paid by another drawn with the sword, as it was said three thousand years ago, so still it must be said, 'the judgments of the Lord, are true and righteous altogether.' "[38]

"Interpretive Anarchy" versus the Rule of Law?

Law professors Larry Alexander and Frederick Schauer have offered the most sophisticated recent defense of judicial supremacy.[39] They argue that the rule of law requires that people refrain from making independent judgments about what the Constitution requires. People must accept without examination the interpretations provided by what Alexander and Schauer call a "single authoritative decisionmaker." Otherwise, they argue, a regime of "interpretive anarchy" will leave people unable to coordinate their actions in matters on which they disagree. And coordination is important so that people can go about their lives without continually reopening matters that are settled in ways they can live with, though they might prefer them to be settled with some other result. Law can coordinate behavior effectively only if people follow the authoritative decision maker's decision. Alexander and Schauer suggest that the courts, and particularly the Supreme Court, serve this "settlement function" of law. Allowing public officials to act on a constitutional interpretation different from the one provided by the Supreme Court would introduce an undesir-

40

settlement function works w/ a single authoritative interpreter.

able degree of instability. The settlement function can be performed well only if there is "a single authoritative interpreter to which others must defer." Alexander and Schauer thus defend judicial supremacy.

Or so it might seem. On closer examination, however, Alexander and Schauer actually defend a much weaker proposition, one entirely compatible with the analysis I have provided. Alexander and Schauer appear to argue that the rule of law entails their version of judicial supremacy to ensure the stability necessary to guarantee that the law's settlement function will be performed acceptably. But their argument actually supports a rather different conclusion. What they establish is that the rule of law entails that a legal system have a set of institutional arrangements sufficient to ensure that degree of stability necessary to guarantee that the law's settlement function will be performed acceptably.

Perhaps, as Alexander and Schauer put it in their conclusion, "at times good institutional design requires norms that compel decision makers to defer to the judgments of others with which they disagree." The question regarding judicial supremacy is, "Who are the decision makers and who are the others?" Nothing in Alexander and Schauer's formal argument precludes the conclusion that "at times good institutional design requires norms that compel [Supreme Court justices] to defer to the judgments of [Congress] with which they disagree." Rather, everything would seem to turn on the question of what a good institutional design is, a question that Alexander and Schauer address only in a long footnote.[40] Their argument there begins by conceding that the single authoritative interpreter could be Congress.

why Supreme Ct. & not Congress as single authoritative interpreter

Alexander and Schauer then offer several reasons why the Supreme Court is preferable to Congress as the single authoritative interpreter.[41] One is that the settlement function requires stability "over time as well as across institutions," and that courts respect the principle of *stare decisis* while legislatures do not. And yet, as Alexander and Schauer realize, the Supreme Court acknowledges its power to overrule its precedents more readily in constitutional law than elsewhere. In 1991 the Supreme Court overruled an important death penalty precedent it had announced only four years earlier; in 1997 it overruled an important establishment clause precedent decided twelve years before.[42] And, of course, decisions regularly modify or undermine precedents in ways that open up new vistas for constitutional transformation.

All this weakens the claim that the Supreme Court is a uniquely stable source of authoritative decisions, particularly when it is coupled with the instabilities that randomly timed appointments to the Supreme Court introduce. In addition, Alexander and Schauer assert that legislatures and executives are less bound by principles of precedent. That may be true, although it probably underestimates the possibility that legislatures are regulated by norms prescribing that it is generally a good thing to do things the way they have been done before.

In any event, the question for institutional design is not what *principles* govern the institutions, but what *practices* they engage in. Here Alexander and Schauer's inattention to empirical questions seems particularly damaging to their argument. Legislative inertia is a powerful force in general, which means that a legislative solution once arrived at is likely to persist for a reasonably long time. Of course there are examples of short-term oscillations in legislative policy, but then, so too are there examples of short-term oscillations in judicial doctrine. Only an empirical investigation could tell us whether such oscillations, particularly on fundamental questions, are more common in courts or legislatures. Partly because of Congress's deference to the Supreme Court, we have relatively few examples of statutes addressing fundamental constitutional questions. But my guess is that any such statutes would have at least as long a shelf life as the Supreme Court's constitutional decisions.[43]

What, then, does "good institutional design" require of institutions to ensure the degree of stability sufficient to guarantee that law's settlement function will be performed acceptably across institutions and over time? It almost certainly does not *require* judicial supremacy in any strong form. As Jeremy Waldron has put it, what reason could we have to think that a rule requiring deference to the judgments of five people, who are replaced at random intervals, produces more stability than a rule requiring deference to the judgments of a majority of the House of Representatives and the Senate, ordinarily with the concurrence of the president? Or, those bothered by the unrealistic prospect of dramatic short-term shifts in a purely majoritarian system in which power is divided among several institutions whose members are elected by majorities or, sometimes, pluralities, and serve varying terms of office, should consider the following rule of institutional design: the Supreme Court's interpretations of the Constitution prevail in general, unless they are rejected by wide majorities in both houses of Congress. This rule rejects judicial supremacy in one area, to some extent, but I believe there is no reason whatever to think that it fails to satisfy the entailments of the rule of law that Alexander and Schauer identify.

We can deepen our understanding of Alexander and Schauer's argument by considering another possibility, more in the domain of political science than law. The argument here begins by noting the inaccuracy of saying, as Alexander and Schauer do, that the Supreme Court is the "single authoritative decisionmaker" their account of the rule of law requires. But, of course, "the Supreme Court" is actually an institution, whose decision-making rule is, "Majority vote among nine individual members." In Alexander and Schauer's usage, a "single" authoritative decision maker cannot possibly be one person. It is an institution, located, in their view, in one building in Washington, D.C. But if a "single" decision maker can be a group of people who work in one building, why can't a "single" decision maker be a group of people who work in two buildings—the Supreme Court building and the national Congress across the street?

Alexander and Schauer's conceptual analysis establishes the need for an institution of authoritative decision making. But institutions are complex patterns of regular behavior, not single individuals—as their example of the Supreme Court demonstrates—or even aggregates of individuals who happen to work in the same building. Whether the Court actually is supreme will be determined by a complex and extended process of interbranch interaction, and that interaction constitutes an institution that is the single authoritative decision maker that the rule of law requires, according to Alexander and Schauer. All that is needed is enough stability to allow the law's settlement function to be performed. And, I believe, it would be impossible to establish that the complex system of interbranch interaction, in which members in each branch make their own decisions about what the Constitution requires, would be any more unstable than the system of judicial supremacy.[44]

THE IDEA OF A THIN CONSTITUTION

The rule of law, then, does not require judicial supremacy. But, I have argued, good institutional design may require good political leadership. Emphasizing political leadership focuses on a procedural dimension of the question of identifying the people's vital interests. Emphasizing Lincoln's role in the Civil War focuses on a substantive dimension.[45]

Political scientist Gary Jacobsohn has helpfully retrieved an obscure note written by Lincoln, in which Lincoln described "[t]he Union and the Constitution" as "the picture of silver," the "frame," around the "apple of gold," the principles of the Declaration of Independence: "The picture was made for the apple— not the apple for the picture."[46] The project the Constitution established for the people of the United States, Lincoln believed, was the vindication of the Declaration's principles: the principle that all people were created equal, the principle that all had inalienable rights. I call this the *thin* Constitution, not because its principles are unimportant—indeed, I believe they are the only important ones in the Constitution—but to contrast it with the thick Constitution containing many details about how to organize the national government and many principles, including much of the Bill of Rights, that attempt to specify what the Declaration's principles mean in particular contexts.

I use the formulations I have—replacing "men" with "people," omitting the Declaration's statement that people were "endowed by their Creator" with inalienable rights—to emphasize that the project is vindicating *principles*. Those principles may differ from

44

the interpretation Thomas Jefferson had: the principle of equality encompasses all people even though Jefferson referred only to men and owned slaves.[47] They may be justified on grounds other than the ones Jefferson had: the principle of rights can rest on secular grounds even though Jefferson offered a deistic justification.

Frederick Douglass's comment on the Dred Scott decision restated these points helpfully. He focused on the Constitution's first words—"We the People." Douglass said, "'We, the people'—not we, the white people—not we, the citizens, or the legal voters—not we, the privileged class, and excluding all other classes but we, the people; not we, the horses and cattle, but we the people—the men and women, the human inhabitants of the United States, do ordain and establish this Constitution."[48] As Douglass understood, the national project includes vindicating the parts of the Constitution's preamble that resonate with the Declaration: the nation's commitment to "establish Justice, ensure domestic Tranquility, provide for the common defense, promote the general Welfare, and secure the Blessings of Liberty to . . . our posterity."

As Lincoln saw it, the Constitution should be interpreted to advance the Declaration's project, when its terms were fairly open to such an interpretation. Public officials should take advancing the project as a "political rule." The Constitution should be amended as quickly as political circumstances made possible, if its provisions impeded the project. And a political leader can provoke a constitutional crisis when political circumstances make it impossible to advance the nation's project. Challenged during the Civil War that his suspension of the writ of habeas corpus was unconstitutional, Lincoln noted that the secessionist South was resisting "the whole of the laws," and said, "Are all the laws but one to go unexecuted, and the Government itself go to pieces, lest that one be violated?"[49]

Both the substantive and the procedural requirements are important, if only because the Declaration's principles are not self-interpreting. Justice Clarence Thomas believes that the Declaration's principle of equality invalidates race-based affirmative action programs, for example, while his adversaries believe that the same principle justifies such programs.[50] This analysis leaves open a wide range in which public officials—with sufficient leadership ability—can reject the general theory of judicial supremacy without undermining the nation's most fundamental commitments even if they thereby do provoke a constitutional crisis.

The range is not infinite, however. Law professor Geoffrey Miller suggests that a president or legislator can provoke a constitutional crisis by defying the courts when doing so is necessary to preserve an energetic government with sufficient effective power to address the nation's pressing problems.[51] Perhaps defiance may be appropriate only when the Declaration's human rights principles are at stake—or, more narrowly, when the president's or legislator's position does not contradict those principles.

A remark by President Andrew Jackson provides a good example of the limits. In the 1820s and 1830s Jackson supported the state of Georgia's efforts to force the Cherokee Indians from the state. Among other moves, Georgia made it a crime for a non-Indian to live on Cherokee land. It prosecuted Samuel Worcester, a missionary, for doing so. Eventually the case got to the Supreme Court, which held the Georgia statute unconstitutional.[52] An unconfirmed story has President Jackson saying, "John Marshall has made his decision; now let him enforce it."[53] Had Jackson actually defied a Supreme Court judgment against him, he would have been wrong. A defender of Georgia's position might have maintained that removal was necessary to ensure domestic tranquility. The problems of law and order Georgia faced, however, were of its own making, not the Cherokees'. And defiance in support of Georgia's racist Indian removal policy would contradict the Declaration's principles.

Even more strongly, Governor Faubus could not plausibly have claimed that his actions advanced the Declaration's project. The most he could establish was that he was acting on behalf of states' rights, which he might connect to the Preamble by citing its first purpose, "to form a more perfect union." I omitted that purpose from my earlier quotation of the Preamble precisely because it does not resonate with the Declaration's principles as the other purposes recited in the Preamble do. The Constitution's detailed arrangements regarding federalism, states' rights, and the separation of powers are the frame of silver that was made for the apple of gold.

The role the Declaration's principles plays in the analysis shows why someone who rejects judicial supremacy does not thereby defend an anarchic system in which the law is whatever anyone thinks it ought to be. The Declaration's principles define our fundamental law. Vigorous disagreement over what those principles mean for any specific problem of public policy does not mean that we as a society have no fundamental law in common.

Douglass. Declaration of independence

VOTERS AND THE THIN CONSTITUTION

So far we have considered the limits, if any, on a public official's disregard of controlling Supreme Court opinions. What of ordinary citizens?[54]

The first point to note is that native-born citizens do not typically have to take an oath to uphold the Constitution, as public officials and naturalized citizens do. An ordinary citizen does not break faith with any duty he or she has undertaken if the citizen ignores what the Supreme Court has said, even if the Supreme Court's interpretations of the Constitution are the supreme law of the land. A public official asked to enforce Proposition 187 faces a problem: "I swore to uphold the Constitution, and the Supreme Court has said that its constitutional interpretations are the supreme law of the land and that a key part of Proposition 187 is unconstitutional. How can I reconcile enforcing that part with the oath I took?" In contrast, a California voter entering the booth to vote on Proposition 187 could say, "I'm going to vote for it even though I know the Supreme Court has said that a key part of it is unconstitutional. What's that to me?"[55]

We might call this a mild form of civil disobedience. The term is slightly out of place. The citizen is disobeying the Supreme Court, but in the service of the law as the citizen sees it. Most constitutional theorists believe that even stronger forms of civil disobedience are sometimes justified, again in the service of law even though the person may be disobeying a specific statute or disregarding a specific Supreme Court decision. Civil disobedience has its costs, which a prudent citizen would take into account before deciding to engage in it. We saw, however, that the case for legislative and executive actions inconsistent with a general theory of judicial supremacy could take such costs into account without difficulty.

At this point in the argument, liberals might raise the specter of the Second Amendment. The relevant judicial opinions uniformly hold that the Second Amendment does not protect an individual's right to own guns. The cases say that the amendment's explanatory preface—"A well-regulated Militia, being necessary to the security of a free State"—shows that the right to bear arms implicates only the right of state governments to organize collective measures of social protection. Academic opinion is divided, but recently something close to a consensus has emerged that the judicial understanding is wrong, and that the amendment really does create an individual right.[56]

The "individual right" view is widely held by the American people as well. Does the argument that ordinary citizens can generally ignore the courts' constitutional interpretations mean that there is nothing problematic about that fact? In the end, it does. But there is some work to do before we reach the end.

Once again we must turn to the Declaration and the Preamble. Unlike Governor Faubus, proponents of the "individual right" interpretation of the Second Amendment can plausibly connect their position to the Preamble: individual ownership of guns helps ensure domestic tranquility, and it may be necessary under contemporary conditions as a method of controlling a government that routinely disregards the people's rights, which the Declaration says would justify armed resistance. Proponents of gun control of course think otherwise. In their view, private ownership of guns enhances the risk of crime and civil disorder. This is no different from the disagreement between Justice Thomas and his adversaries about the Declaration's meaning. If that disagreement raises no fundamental questions about our constitutional order, neither should this one.

There is a deeper point. In my view, constitutional law rests on a commitment to democracy, a commitment itself embodied in the Declaration's principles. No one can guarantee that democratic processes will always yield results I agree with. Reasonable people can disagree with the judgments I make about what the Declaration's principles require. Democracy is a way of resolving such disagreements without routinely risking severe social disorder. Of course, if democracy regularly produced disagreeable results, or occasionally produced truly vile ones, I would rethink my commitment to democracy. But the simple fact that on some issues people would adopt policies—or constitutional interpretations—I disagree with is hardly bothersome. It establishes instead that if I care enough I ought to try to persuade people that a different policy would better advance the Declaration's project.

Does this mean that an ordinary citizen can disregard not just Supreme Court decisions but the Constitution itself? The answer is, "No." Ordinary citizens ought to continue the Declaration's project—and therefore ought to take the Constitution into account when it advances that project—in part because the Declaration's principles state unassailable moral truths. At least as important, however, the nation's commitment to the Declaration's project constitutes us as the people of the United States, and constituting a people is a morally worthy project.[57]

NOTES

1. 5 U.S. (1 Cranch) 137 (1803).

2. 457 U.S. 202 (1982).

3. League of United Latin American Citizens v. Wilson, 908 F.Supp. 755 (C.D. Cal. 1995) (noting that it had temporarily enjoined relevant provisions of Proposition 187 one week after its effective date).

4. Employment Division, Department of Human Resources v. Smith, 494 U.S. 872 (1990).

5. City of Boerne v. Flores, 117 S.Ct. 2157, 2172 (1997).

6. 358 U.S. 1 (1958).

7. 60 U.S. (17 How.) 393 (1857).

8. THE LINCOLN-DOUGLAS DEBATES OF 1858 (Edwin Erle Sparks ed. 1908), 257, 372.

9. 2 COLLECTED WORKS OF ABRAHAM LINCOLN (Roy Basler ed. 1953), 516, 518.

10. First Inaugural Address, March 4, 1861, 6 MESSAGES AND PAPERS OF THE PRESIDENTS (J. Richardson ed. 1897), 9.

11. The Civil War crisis elicited Lincoln's analysis, but he gave reasons that are available in more ordinary situations.

12. Frank Easterbrook, *Presidential Review,* 40 CASE WESTERN RES. L.REV. 905 (1989–90), deals with the issues raised in this section rather more casually than they deserve. He reaches conclusions generally compatible with mine, although without working through some of the complications.

13. Jefferson to Abigail Adams, Sept. 11, 1804, in 11 WRITINGS OF THOMAS JEFFERSON (Albert E. Bergh ed. 1905), 311–13.

14. The Supreme Court itself never ruled on the act's constitutionality, but Jefferson did not appear to think that this is an important analytic feature of the problem.

15. Veto Message, July 10, 1832, in 2 MESSAGES AND PAPERS OF THE PRESIDENTS (J. Richardson ed. 1897), 576–91.

16. Barzilai v. Government of Israel (The General Security Service Pardon Case), SELECTED JUDGMENTS OF THE SUPREME COURT OF ISRAEL, vol. 6 (Jerusalem: Supreme Court of Israel, 1986), suggests that that Court would review presidential pardons using a standard like "unreasonableness."

17. This latter course is not entirely satisfactory. A president whose decision to veto was controlled by constitutional concerns—either entirely or enough to tip the balance against a bill about which the president had policy doubts—might send a veto message expressing only policy concerns.

18. E. C. MASON, THE VETO POWER (Albert Bushnell Hart ed. 1891), 129.

19. The Senate has a procedure that might be used more widely than it has been. Under the Senate's rules, a senator can raise a question of constitutionality, which must be submitted to the Senate as a whole for resolution. Policy debate ends when such a motion is made. Senators then may discuss only constitutional questions. If the motion succeeds—that is, if the Senate believes that the proposal is unconstitutional—the underlying legislative proposal is defeated. If the motion fails, the Senate turns back to policy questions.

What would happen if this procedure were widely used in both houses of Congress? If Congress enacts the bill, it is subject to judicial review. Suppose the Senate or the House accepts the motion, finding the proposal unconstitutional. It is not hard to see how a constitutional system could still provide judicial review, although we might have to change some details of the Supreme Court's holdings about who can raise constitutional challenges to get to this point. Perhaps a legislator who voted *against* the motion could ask the courts whether the legislative majority's view of the Constitution was right. If the courts said the majority was wrong, the effect would be the same as defeating the motion of unconstitutionality: Congress would then go back to discussing only the proposal's policy dimensions

The French constitutional system does use motions of unconstitutionality. Two points about the French practice deserve note here. First, they almost never succeed, because of the structure of party politics in the French legislature: from 1958 to 1984, ninety-six motions were made, seventy-one were voted on, and only one passed. Second, the use of the motion has grown as the French Constitutional Council has expanded its own reach.

20. Michael Stokes Paulsen, *The* Merryman *Power and the Dilemma of Autonomous Executive Branch Interpretation*, 15 CARDOZO L.REV. 81 (1993), 100.

21. Technically, President Jefferson could not have prosecuted people for violating the antisedition act, which had expired according to a sunset provision before he took office. The analytic point I make is, however, still available, but harder to state as concisely as the version in the text.

22. Courts have in fact upheld denial of publicly funded nonemergency medical care even to aliens legally present in the country.

23. Coker v. Georgia, 433 U.S. 584 (1977).

24. Stanford v. Kentucky, 492 U.S. 361 (1989).

25. There are other ways: enact a statute purportedly distinguishable and hope that the Court will say, "This case is actually not distinguishable from our precedent, which we hereby overrule." Here the legislator has to hope that the Court will bite the bullet; in the case involving a reenacted statute already held unconstitutional, the Court has no choice.

26. Texas v. Hopwood, 116 S.Ct. 2581 (1996). The original court of appeals opinion is at 78 F.3d 932 (5th Cir. 1996).

27. After the Supreme Court denied review, attorneys for the Texas plaintiffs asserted that officials and schools that continued to take race

into account risked liability for punitive damages. Where there is a reasonable basis for believing that a test case would succeed, and when race is taken into account to provide the basis for such a case, I doubt that punitive damages would actually be available.

28. Minersville School Dist. v. Gobitis, 310 U.S. 586 (1940).

29. West Virginia Board of Education v. Barnette, 319 U.S. 624 (1943). The head counting is done in the lower court opinion, 47 F. Supp. 251 (S.D. W.Va. 1942).

30. *See, e.g.*, Evan H. Caminker, *Precedent and Prediction: The Forward-Looking Aspects of Inferior Court Decisionmaking*, 73 TEX. L.REV. 1, 22–23 (1994) (describing but not endorsing these concerns).

31. Planned Parenthood of Southeast Pennsylvania v. Casey, 505 U.S. 833 (1992).

32. Texas v. Johnson, 491 U.S. 397 (1989); United States v. Eichman, 496 U.S. 310 (1990). More precisely, the Court held such statutes unconstitutional when they outlawed flag burning as an expression of opposition to public policy.

33. That majority has been unable to effectuate its preferences because doing so would require amending the Constitution, and the majority may not be the supermajority—represented by two-thirds in both houses of Congress and by majorities in legislatures of three-fourths of the states—that the Constitution requires for a constitutional amendment. Alternatively, the majority may be the requisite supermajority among the people, but finds its desires obstructed by opposition from within the political elites who are members of Congress.

34. Of course, precisely because dismissal is certain, the costs to the defendant will not be that great.

35. Daniel Patrick Moynihan, "What do you do when the Supreme Court is wrong?" *The Public Interest*, 1979, no. 2, 3.

36. I draw my account of *Merryman* from Paulsen, *supra* note 20, 89–91.

37. Edwin Meese III, *The Law of the Constitution*, 61 TULANE L.REV. 979 (1987).

38. Second Inaugural Address, March 4, 1865, 6 MESSAGES AND PAPERS OF THE PRESIDENTS (J. Richardson ed. 1897), 277.

39. Larry Alexander and Frederick Schauer, *On Extrajudicial Constitutional Interpretation*, 110 HARV. L.REV. 1359 (1997).

40. One might think that questions about institutional design are fundamentally empirical. Oddly, Alexander and Schauer say that their analysis "is neither empirical nor historical." *Id.* at 1369.

41. One simply restates the issue: "[T]here is little reason to believe that a legislature or an executive is best situated to determine the contours of the constraints on its own power." True enough, but equally true as to the Supreme Court.

42. Payne v. Tennessee, 501 U.S. 808 (1991); Agostini v. Felton, 117 S.Ct. 1997 (1997).

43. Alexander and Schauer's final reason for preferring the Supreme Court to Congress as the single authoritative interpreter is that "constitutions are designed to guard against the excesses of majoritarian forces that influence legislatures and executives more than they influence courts." This is an important assertion, which I question in detail elsewhere, where I argue that "majoritarian forces" influence courts no less than they influence legislatures and executives, though they influence them in a different way and on a somewhat different timetable. For a short version of the argument, see Mark Tushnet, "Is Judicial Review Good for the Left?" DISSENT, December 1997.

44. Some of Alexander and Schauer's discussion gets off on the wrong foot by failing to attend to the difference between the behavior of legal institutions, which is what their analysis is really about, and the decision-making processes of individuals within those institutions. As long as the institutions ensure reasonably stable legal decisions, it is irrelevant on their analysis whether particular individuals arrive at their own independent judgments about what the Constitution means. Notably, sometimes, perhaps often, a person's independent constitutional analysis will lead him or her to agree with the Court's interpretation. And nearly every Court decision has *some* constituency to support it, which provides a check on wild oscillations in policy.

45. The otherwise excellent treatment in Michael Stokes Paulsen, *The Most Dangerous Branch: Executive Power to Say What the Law Is*, 83 GEO. L.J. 217 (1994), is flawed because it overlooks these procedural and substantive issues. Another recent overview of the issues discussed here is Scott E. Gant, *Judicial Supremacy and Nonjudicial Interpretation of the Constitution*, 24 HASTINGS CONST. L.Q. 359 (1997).

46. GARY JACOBSOHN, APPLE OF GOLD: CONSTITUTIONALISM IN ISRAEL AND THE UNITED STATES 3 (1993) (quoting Lincoln; emphasis omitted).

47. The distinction is familiar to legal academics from Ronald Dworkin. RONALD DWORKIN, TAKING RIGHTS SERIOUSLY 134–35 (1977).

48. Frederick Douglass, "The Dred Scott Decision," in 2 LIFE AND WRITINGS OF FREDERICK DOUGLASS (Philip S. Foner ed., 1950–55), 419.

49. Special Session Message, July 4, 1861, 6 MESSAGES AND PAPERS OF

THE PRESIDENTS (J. Richardson ed. 1897), 25. Lincoln proceeded to defend the suspension as justified within the Constitution. He was willing to provoke a constitutional crisis, that is, but did not believe he had actually done so.

50. *Compare* Adarand Constructors, Inc. v. Pena, 515 U.S. 200, 240 (1995) (Thomas, J., concurring) (citing the Declaration of Independence), *with* Regents of the University of California v. Bakke, 438 U.S. 265, 407 (1978) (Blackmun, J., concurring) ("In order to get beyond racism, we must take account of race").

51. Geoffrey P. Miller, *The President's Power of Interpretation: Implications of a Unified Theory of Constitutional Law,* 56 LAW & CONTEMP. PROB. no. 4 (1993), 35.

52. Worcester v. Georgia, 31 U.S. (6 Pet.) 515 (1832).

53. In fact, Georgia acquiesced in the Court's decision, although with some hesitation; eventually the state's governor pardoned Worcester. *See* G. EDWARD WHITE, THE MARSHALL COURT AND CULTURAL CHANGE, 1815–35 (1988), 737–39.

54. A different set of issues arises when Congress and the president disagree about the Constitution's meaning—for example, when the president refuses to enforce a law enacted over a presidential veto because the president believes it to be unconstitutional. I deal with this problem in the larger work of which this chapter is a part.

55. There is some reason to believe that some voters voted in favor of Proposition 187 because they had been convinced that it was *un*constitutional. It would not have the dire effects its opponents predicted, and voters could express their disapproval of illegal immigration without having to worry that their actions would have real consequences. See David Sklansky, *Proposition 187 and the Ghost of James Bradley Thayer,* 17 CHICANO-LATINO L.REV. 24, 36–39 (1995).

56. For a survey presenting the consensus view, see Glenn Harlan Reynolds, *A Critical Guide to the Second Amendment,* 62 TENN. L.REV. 461 (1995). For a critique, see Garry Wills, "To Keep and Bear Arms," New York Rev. of Books, Sept. 21, 1995, p. 62. The article that opened the issue for law professors is Sanford Levinson, *The Embarrassing Second Amendment,* 99 YALE L.J. 639 (1989). For an overview of the judicial interpretations, see Andrew Herz, *Gun Crazy: Constitutional False Consciousness and Dereliction of Dialogic Responsibility,* 75 B.U. L.REV. 57 (1995).

57. Again, I develop this argument in more detail elsewhere.

CHAPTER TWO

"Despotism in Some Form":
Marbury v. Madison

JEREMY WALDRON

I'M ALMOST CERTAINLY the wrong person to offer critical comments on Mark Tushnet's chapter, for I am so much in agreement with the overall project, as well as much of the detail of his presentation, that my main reaction is to call for more of the same.

Tushnet's general thesis, I take it, is that the U.S. Constitution belongs to the people, in a sense that is not just rhetorical and not just a matter of provenance—who wrote it and who ratified it—but rather in the sense that it "belongs to the people" which is sufficiently robust to raise questions about the doctrine of judicial supremacy. This thesis, Tushnet thinks, ought to have some considerable impact on our understanding of the authority and responsibilities of the various branches of government, particularly in our understanding of the relations between the executive and the courts, and between the legislature and the courts, both at state and federal levels.

No one doubts, of course, that it is the task of the courts to hear and determine particular cases and controversies among particular litigants, and that their determinations should be authoritative and, at the level of the highest court, final and dispositive—*of the particular case*. No one doubts that this should be so even when the particular case or controversy has a constitutional dimension. But Tushnet is arguing that there is some considerable distance between that proposition and the proposition that it is for the courts to say finally what the Constitution means and what it requires. The latter proposition is not one that he is prepared to accept, particularly if it implies some tentativeness or lack of authority or a less than final standing in the deliberations and decisions of the other institutions of government that, in their structure, ethos, and accountability, purport to represent—more directly than the courts do—the people whose Constitution this is.

I don't want to put words into Tushnet's mouth, but as I understand it, he rejects the view that the people or their representatives never have the standing to authoritatively interpret or revise the interpretation of the Constitution except in the process of formally amending it, except in the course of the extraordinary procedures laid down in Article 5 of the Constitution itself. I think he wants to reject the view—the common view—which holds that, so far as *ordinary* politics is concerned, the courts, particularly the Supreme Court, are the only branch of government entrusted with the task of keeping the Constitution up-to-date. Let me explain what I mean by the last phrase.

It is sometimes said that a Constitution is not a dead document, but something more animate. In the words of Justice Louis Brandeis, it is "a living organism . . . capable of growth—of expansion and of adaptation to new conditions."[1] If we regard the U.S. Constitution in that light, then since it will not change and adapt by itself or by magic, we have to ask: "Who (or which organs of government) should be empowered to participate in this organic process of change and adaptation?" Certainly the courts must; that will be part and parcel of the responsibility to determine particular cases. But who else must, in the ordinary run of things? If it is really necessary for society, in the words of Justice Brennan, "to adapt canons of right to situations not envisaged by those who framed them, thereby facilitating their evolution and preserving their vitality,"[2] why should the legislature or the executive be excluded—or, more correctly, why should they be excluded in all circumstances except the circumstance in which they manage to get themselves into a formal Article 5 amending mode? As things stand, the courts seem to be accorded the power to change the current authoritative understanding of what the Constitution means and requires, and they are empowered to do that as part and parcel of their ordinary business of hearing and determining particular cases. We have accustomed ourselves to take that for granted. Why, then, do we have so much difficulty—and here I am still putting words into Tushnet's mouth—with the notion that the legislature and executive agencies, too, might be empowered to change the current, authoritative understanding of what the Constitution means and requires as part and parcel of *their* ordinary business?

Of course, it is not a matter of anyone amending the Constitution to that effect, or *announcing* that from now on, Congress and the president, or state legislatures and governors, shall be authorized to adapt and interpret the Constitution. It's more a question of why particular patterns of deference have developed, why the political culture of this country has one flavor rather than another. When state legislatures showed, for example, by their persistent activity in passing legislation governing working hours or setting a minimum wage or regulating factory conditions, that they had a new understanding of what was constitutionally appropriate or inappropriate in the governance of economic activity, why is it not natural for a Supreme Court justice to say, "Gosh, things have changed. The Constitution is clearly being read by the people and their representatives in a way that renders the reading I have traditionally preferred obsolete. Maybe I should defer to the new reading, because it is, after all, *their* Constitution." We expect our legislators to say this to themselves all the time about new readings coming from the court, even in situations where the matter has patently come before the courts as a test case for the general proposition, rather than on account of any really urgent necessity to determine some particular case or controversy. Nothing seems more natural to us than that the opponents of some bill or measure will transfer their energies to the court if they are defeated in the legislature, scrambling to find some appropriate plaintiff to eke out their satisfaction of the "case or controversy" requirement. And if they win in court, we expect the legislators to roll over and refrain from passing any similar measure in the future. That's all commonplace in America. Why does the opposite pattern of deference seem so unnatural?

So far all I have been doing is putting words into Tushnet's mouth. But I have put the matter as I have—in terms of "Who gets to change our understanding of the Constitution as part of ordinary politics?"—because I sense that Tushnet is reluctant to have the doctrine of judicial supremacy challenged apart from exceptional cases or in cases of constitutional crisis.

Much of his analysis is devoted to the question, "How do you know when you're in a constitutional crisis? When is an interest 'vital' enough, or what is it for a situation to be extraordinary enough for a president, a governor, or a legislature to be entitled to ignore some judicial pronouncement as to what the Constitution must (now) be taken to mean?" Why "crisis"? Why "vital"? Why "extraordinary"? Why should it not be part of the ordinary separation and interaction of the powers of our government, that, apart from the particular outcome of the particular case on which the Court has ruled, legislatures and governors should show the same healthy disrespect for the Supreme Court's general view of the Constitution as the Supreme Court justices characteristically show for what they take to be the general views of the legislatures?

In answering this question, Tushnet takes his cue from Lincoln's First Inaugural Address. Here the great man objected to the idea that "the policy of the government, *upon vital questions,* is to be irrevocably fixed by decisions of the Supreme Court, the instant they are made in ordinary litigation between parties, in personal actions."[3] He would say Lincoln emphasizes that he is opposed to this happening "upon vital questions." But we must be careful not to read this too legalistically. He may not be saying "if and only if a vital interest is involved"; he may not be laying down a condition; he may be saying instead that the idea of judicial supremacy is objectionable generally, objectionable whenever it is asserted, but particularly objectionable when it is foisted on the people in a case where some vital interest is involved.

If that's the way we read what Lincoln was saying, then we don't have to interpret "vital question" as a necessary condition. We also don't have to embark on a quest for some definition of which issues are vital and which ones are not, appealing to the Preamble and the Declaration of Independence and so on. All that search for criteria of "vitalness" would be unnecessary. Instead, we would have the much simpler doctrine—much more consonant, I think, with the overall argument that Lincoln was making—that the court's dictating policy and principle to the government in general terms is always objectionable, and the more vital the questions involved, the more objectionable it is.

One would be hard put to say that a piece of legislation regarding working hours in Colorado in 1890 engages a vital interest of the nation; it is politics as usual. But there still seems to me some effrontery (of the sort Lincoln was complaining about) in a court imposing upon the state the *judges'* conception—or worse still, the conception of a bare majority of the judges—of when a legislature may and may not legislate on economic matters, rejecting out of hand the view on the constitutional question that the representatives of the people have come up with.

I suspect that Tushnet's caution in this matter has to do with his sense that a government agency taking a stand against a court's view of the Constitution comes dangerously close to direct disobedience to a judicial order, and therefore it's a power which, even if legitimate, ought to be used only in extremis, lest it encourage a general culture of defying the law. There's something to that. Even if we observe the distinction between accepting the court's determination of the case between the particular litigants who have come before it and its more general pronouncements on the Constitution, there still would be dangerous arrogance in the government, say, ending what the court has described as the unconstitutional treatment of X but sticking with similar treatment of Y and Z even though their cases are evidently indistinguishable. There would be something dangerous and unprincipled about that, and opposition along those lines to the court's general interpretation of the constitution would not be something an agency should embark on lightly. Tushnet has given us a subtle and intriguing account of what "taking care" in these circumstances should amount to. But that still leaves the broader point of whether we should concede to the court the power to make what are really general pronouncements on the Constitution and what it means, and have those pronouncements accepted and deferred to, as a matter of course, in ordinary, noncrisis areas of politics. That's what I am not convinced of. I'm not sure that Tushnet is trying to convince us of it; but at any rate I'd like to hear more.

Talk of *disobedience* raises a slightly different issue. Toward the end of his argument, Tushnet said: "So far we have considered the limits, if any, on a public official's disregard of controlling Supreme Court opinions. What," he asks, "of ordinary citizens?" May an ordinary citizen disregard a Supreme Court decision, disobeying a piece of legislation, for example, that the citizen judges unconstitutional even though the Court has determined that it should not be struck down? Can we move from intragovernmental defiance to a more general theory of civil disobedience?

The case for an affirmative answer was made in an early essay by Ronald Dworkin entitled "Civil Disobedience," originally published (like almost everything else Dworkin has written) in the *New York Review of Book* in 1976 and collected in *Taking Rights Seriously*:

> A citizen's allegiance is to the law, not to any particular person's view of what the law is, and he does not behave unfairly so long as he proceeds on his own considered and reasonable view of what the law requires.
>
> . . . [T]his is not the same as saying that an individual may disregard what the courts have said. . . . But if the issue is one touching fundamental personal or political rights and it is arguable that the Supreme Court has made a mistake, a man is within his social rights in refusing to accept that decision as conclusive.[4]

Why the reference in Dworkin's position to issues "touching fundamental personal or political rights"? Isn't this "vital questions" all over again? Actually, his reference to rights at this point does do some work. If someone were to object that when citizens follow their own views about what the Constitution requires, this would lead to disorder or at least to a less orderly situation in which everyone tamely submitted to the Court's view, then Dworkin might respond that this is a mere gain in ordinary utility, which is, presumably, trumped by the individual constitutional rights that the protestor believes are involved.

Tushnet's own answer to the question "May the individual citizen disregard a Supreme Court decision?" is—as far as I can tell—negative. "A populist constitutional law," he said, "rests on a commitment to democracy." I take this to mean that the populist approach assigns ownership of the Constitution not to individual persons but to the people, in their collective capacity. Defiance of the Court, then, is most convincingly legitimate when it is done by the people together, through one of the agencies, or assemblies, or institutions of leadership that represent them in their multiplicity and collectivity.[5] The reason has to do with the prospect of disagreement. Tushnet says this (it's in the context of his use of the Declaration of Independence as a criterion of "vital questions"—which I have already criticized; but for "Declaration" you can read "Constitution"): "No one can guarantee that democratic processes will always yield results that I agree with. I know that reasonable people can disagree with the judgments I make about what the Declaration's principles require. Democracy is a way of resolving such disagreements without routinely risking severe social disorder." The implication is that individual citizens who act idiosyncratically, each on his own particular interpretation, might introduce disorder into our social and political life.

Now, I happen to agree with this, and I *don't* think it's answered by Dworkin's point that disorder is something we just have to accept if it is arguable that fundamental rights are at stake. *In extremis*, that's true. But Tushnet is talking about normal constitutional practice—at least this is what I am trying to push him toward—not about the extremities of rights violations. The point is, we set up a constitution, with its myriad structures, institutions, and decision procedures, because we want the capacity to act together as a people on various issues in spite of our disagreements. The whole point of a constitution—the whole point of political procedures—is to enable us to do that. Now, an understanding of the Constitution is one of the many things we disagree about, and we need the capacity to act on one coherent understanding even though we may disagree about what it should be. So how are we to arrive at that one understanding? One answer is the traditional court-centered answer: the one understanding we are to work with together, in spite of our disagreements, is the one imposed by the Supreme Court through the vetoes of its nine quarrelsome and opinionated members. A better answer is the one put forward by Tushnet: Why confine ourselves to the courts? Why not make use of the full range of our decision procedures, particularly those that explicitly purport to represent us as a people? Why not, as Lincoln suggested, use the method of majority decision, among the people or their representatives, on constitutional issues as on others? I know Lincoln is not our prophet, though I have profited from Tushnet's most useful reminder of Lincoln's position on these matters. So let me close with what was said in Lincoln's First Inaugural Address about the determination of constitutional controversies:

> No foresight can anticipate, nor any document of reasonable length contain, express provisions for all possible questions. Shall fugitives from labor be surrendered by national or by State authority? The Constitution does not expressly say. *May* Congress prohibit slavery in the territories? The Constitution does not expressly say.
>
> From questions of this class [Lincoln went on] spring all our constitutional controversies, and we divide upon them into majorities and minorities. If the minority will not acquiesce, the majority must, or the government must cease. There is no other alternative; for continuing the government, is acquiescence on one side or the other. . . . Unanimity is impossible; the rule of a minority, as a permanent arrangement, is wholly inadmissible; so that, rejecting the majority principle, anarchy, or despotism in some form, is all that is left.[6]

And it was under *this* heading—"despotism in some form"—that Lincoln went on to discuss the idea of the Supreme Court's having the final say, indicating his belief that if that were to happen, "the people will have ceased, to be their own rulers, having, to that extent, practically resigned their government, into the hands of that eminent tribunal."[7]

NOTES

1. Justice Louis Brandeis, quoted in William Brennan, "Why Have a Bill of Rights?" *Oxford Journal of Legal Studies* 9 (1989), 426.

2. Brennan, "Why Have a Bill of Rights?" 426. (These are Brennan's own words now, not those of Brandeis.)

3. Abraham Lincoln, "First Inaugural Address," in his *Speeches and Writings 1859–1965* (New York: Library of America, n.d.), 215, at 221.

4. Ronald Dworkin, *Taking Rights Seriously*, rev. ed. (London: Duckworth, 1977), 214–15.

5. This, by the way, is also John Locke's view, in the final chapter of the *Second Treatise*: "The People shall be Judge," not individual persons.

6. Lincoln, "First Inaugural Address," 220.

7. Ibid., 221.

CHAPTER THREE

Dred Scott v. Sandford
and Its Legacy

CASS R. SUNSTEIN

[O]pinions were so various and at first so crude that it was necessary they should be long debated before any uniform system of opinion could be formed. Meantime the minds of the members were changing, and much was to be gained by a yielding and accommodating spirit. . . . [N]o man felt himself obliged to retain his opinion any longer than he was satisfied of their propriety and truth, and was open to the force of argument.

> (*James Madison*)

The spirit of liberty [is that spirit which] is not
too sure that it is right.
> (*Learned Hand*)

$\mathbf{M}$Y TOPICS IN this chapter are the myths that the Dred Scott case created, the myths that Americans have created about it, and the true lessons of the case for three of the great constitutional issues of the current era: affirmative action, homosexuality, and the right to die.

THE CONTINUING RELEVANCE OF *DRED SCOTT*

The Dred Scott case was probably the most important case in the history of the Supreme Court of the United States. Indeed, it was probably the most important constitutional case in the history of any nation and any court. But most of us have little if any sense of what it means or was even about. Even within the legal culture, the case is taught infrequently in constitutional law courses; outside of the legal culture, the case is pretty well forgotten, or at most a footnote in discussions of the Civil War.

We should note right at the outset some of the many remarkable facts about the case.

- *Dred Scott* was the first Supreme Court case since *Marbury v. Madison* invalidating a federal law. Since *Marbury* created judicial review in the context of a denial of jurisdiction, *Dred Scott* might plausibly be said to be the first real exercise of the power of judicial review.

- *Dred Scott* was the first great effort by the Court to take an issue of political morality out of politics. In that sense, it is the great ancestor of many New Deal and Warren Court cases.

- *Dred Scott* was the birthplace of the controversial idea of "substantive due process," used in *Roe v. Wade*, in many important cases endangering the regulatory/welfare state, and in the recent cases involving the "right to die."

- *Dred Scott* was one of the first great cases unambiguously using the "intent of the framers," and in that sense it was the great precursor of the method of Justice Antonin Scalia and Judge Robert Bork.

THREE MYTHS

Let me now identify the great myths involving *Dred Scott*. The first and perhaps most important one was created by the Dred Scott case itself: The myth is that the original Constitution protected, supported, and entrenched slavery. On this view, the Constitution was emphatically pro-slavery. As a legal matter, this is a myth in the simple sense that it is false: the Constitution does not support or entrench slavery.[1] But many people think the myth is true; in fact, Justice Thurgood Marshall, in his remarks about the bicentennial, basically agreed with the *Dred Scott* Court.

The second myth comes from the conventional American "reading" of *Dred Scott*. According to that reading, Chief Justice Roger Taney was a morally obtuse person heading a morally obtuse Court that it took a Civil War to overturn. This is a different kind of myth. It is not exactly false. But it is hardly the full story; it leaves enormous gaps. An adequate understanding of *Dred Scott* lies elsewhere. It has a great deal to do with the appropriate role of the Supreme Court in American government. It has to do with how a democratic citizenry governs itself.

The third myth is a revisionist reading of the case, coming from Justice Scalia and others critical of the Warren Court. Here is myth number 3: *Dred Scott* was wrong because the Court abandoned the "intentions of the framers" in favor of its own conception of social policy. On this view, *Dred Scott* was wrong because it was politics rather than law, and it was politics rather than law because it abandoned the Constitution, understood as a historical document. This myth has more than a kernel of truth in it, for *Dred Scott* cannot be said to have been an accurate reading of the original understanding of the framers. But myth number 3 qualifies as a myth because *Dred Scott* was very much and very self-consciously an "originalist" opinion, that is, it purported to draw nearly all of its support from the views of the framers:

> It is not the province of the court to decide upon the justice or injustice, the policy or impolicy, of these laws. The decision of that question belonged to the political or law-making power; to those who formed the sovereignty and framed the Constitution. The duty of the court is, to interpret the instrument they have framed, with the best lights we can obtain on the subject, and to administer it as we find it, according to its true intent and meaning when it was adopted.[2]

To replace these myths, I suggest that the defect of *Dred Scott* lay largely in the Court's effort to resolve, once and for all time, an issue that was splitting the nation on political and moral grounds. More particularly, we should understand *Dred Scott* to suggest that, in general and if it possibly can,[3] the Supreme Court should avoid political thickets. It should leave Great Questions to politics. This is because the Court may answer those questions incorrectly, and because it may well make things worse even if it answers correctly.

What I will suggest is that the Court should—as the *Dred Scott* Court did not—proceed *casuistically,* and this in two different ways. First, it should generally decide cases rather than set down broad rules. Second, it should try to avoid issues of basic principle and instead attempt to reach *incompletely theorized agreements on particular cases.*[4] By this term I mean concrete judgments on which people can converge from diverse foundations. In this way the Court can both model and promote a crucial goal of a liberal political system: to make it possible for people to agree when agreement is necessary, and to make it unnecessary for people to agree when agreement is impossible.

These claims have a set of implications for contemporary questions. I deal with three such questions here: affirmative action, the right to die, and homosexuality. My unifying theme is that the Court should generally adopt strategies that promote rather than undermine democratic reflection and debate. I suggest, first and in some ways foremost, that courts should not invalidate affirmative action. The court of appeals' decision in the recent *Hopwood* case was hubristic in the same sense as *Dred Scott*—an effort, with insufficient constitutional warrant, to remove a big issue of principle from politics. The attack on affirmative action is a legitimate and in some ways salutary part of political debate; as a legal phenomenon it reflects a form of judicial hubris. At most, the Court should invalidate the most irrational and extreme affirmative action programs, and in that way attempt to promote and to inform democratic deliberation on the underlying issues.

With the right to die, things are a bit different; here the problem is that the relevant laws are old and based on perhaps anachronistic assumptions, and hence the basic issue has not been subject to democratic debate. I suggest that the Court should proceed cautiously, incrementally, on a fact-specific basis. Instead of vindicating a broad "right to privacy," courts might say—if they are to play any role at all—that intrusions on individual liberty may not be based on old laws rooted in different circumstances and perhaps anachronistic values, and that any such intrusions must be supported by more recent acts of political deliberation. For the right to die, the best approach lies in a form of self-conscious dialogue between courts and legislatures.

In some ways the question of discrimination on grounds of sexual orientation is the hardest—at least if one believes, as I do,[5] that such discrimination is generally unacceptable under constitutional principles as they are appropriately understood. I will suggest a form of incrementalism in support of a constitutional attack on discrimination against homosexuals. Even if courts believe that the attack is plausible on its merits, they should hesitate before entering this "political thicket." They should follow President Lincoln, not Chief Justice Taney.

DRED SCOTT: *DRAMATIS PERSONAE*

Every myth is filled with people, usually people of high drama. This is certainly true of the Dred Scott story. Let me tell you something about the people behind the *Dred Scott* case.

Who was Dred Scott? We lack full answers. It appears that he was born in about 1799—around the date of the ratification of the Bill of Rights—and that he was quite short, about five feet tall. His real name may have been Sam. The only picture of Dred Scott, taken in 1856, shows him in his mid-fifties. After interviewing Scott in 1857, a St. Louis newspaper said that Scott was "illiterate but not ignorant" and that he had a strong common sense sharpened by his many travels. There is reason to believe that Scott provided initiative for his case. Immediately before the suit was filed, Scott tried to buy his freedom from his owner, Mrs. Emerson. She declined. The *Dred Scott* case followed.

Since childhood, Scott had lived in Virginia with Peter Blow and his wife, Elizabeth. The Blows moved from Virginia to Alabama and then, in 1830, left with seven children (including Taylor, whose name you should remember) and six slaves for St. Louis, Missouri. This was not a good place for the family: Peter Blow's business venture, the Jefferson Hotel, did poorly; Elizabeth Blow died in 1831; Peter died a year later.

After Peter Blow's death, Dr. John Emerson bought one of his slaves and in 1833 took that slave, Dred Scott, into service at Fort Armstrong in Illinois. Illinois was a nonslave state, and this was important. Scott thus lived for an extended period in a state that outlawed slavery, raising a key question in his case: Was he thereby freed?

In 1838 Emerson took Scott for a second sojourn into Fort Snelling, near what is now St. Paul, Minnesota. Scott, held as a slave in the free state of Illinois for more than two years, was now living in a territory in which slavery was banned by the Missouri Compromise. There Scott met Harriet Robinson, a slave about twenty years old; Harriet was sold to Emerson and she and Scott were married, their marriage lasting until Scott's death in 1858. Four children were born to them; the two sons died as infants, but two daughters (Eliza, born in 1838, and Lizzie, born in 1847) survived and became parties to the *Dred Scott* case. Scott stayed with Emerson until Emerson's death in 1843. John Sanford, Emerson's brother-in-law, was an executor of his will.

Dred Scott had apparently been in the service of Mrs. Irene Emerson's brother-in-law, Captain Bainbridge, from 1843 to 1846. On April 6, 1846, Dred and Harriet Scott brought suit against Irene Emerson, alleging assault and false imprisonment, and complaining that Emerson had beaten and imprisoned Dred. And they claimed that they were free.

It is worth noting at this point that Dred Scott remained friends with the Blow family long after the death of Peter and Elizabeth. The Blows and their in-laws were the Scotts' principal supporters during the lawsuits, which lasted until 1857. We should especially remember Taylor Blow, Dred Scott's benefactor from the day he was freed until the day of his death. Interestingly, Taylor Blow was not opposed to slavery in principle, and apparently acted due to personal bonds extending back to childhood.

These, then, are the people behind the case: Dred, Harriet, Eliza, and Lizzie Scott, the plaintiffs; Peter and Elizabeth Blow, the original owners; Taylor Blow, their son; Irene Emerson and her brother-in-law, John Sanford, the defendants. It should be obvious at this point that a mystery in the *Dred Scott* case is its title: Why was the case styled *Dred Scott v. Sandford*? It could as easily have been called *Harriet Scott v. Emerson*. But as a woman, Harriet Scott could not be the lead plaintiff in a lawsuit, and neither could Irene Emerson be the defendant, so the estate executor replaced her. But the legal interests of both women were emphatically at stake.

Dred Scott: The Law

Now let us turn to the legal issues in the case. Scott noted that the state constitution of Illinois abolished slavery and that the Missouri Compromise banned it in the Louisiana territory. Hence Scott claimed that he was made a free man by virtue of his sustained stays in those places. Sandford responded that Scott was not free, because his former owner had a continuing property interest in him—that is what slavery meant—and because the federal government could not deprive an owner of property without due process of law. Sandford claimed that Scott could not sue in federal court in any case, since Scott was not a citizen of Missouri, or indeed of any state.

The largest question in the case was whether Dred Scott was still a slave, which in turn raised three principal issues.

1. Could Scott sue in federal court? If he were a citizen of Missouri, suing a citizen of New York, he could indeed sue under the diversity of citizenship provision of the federal Constitution, which gives federal courts jurisdiction over disputes between people domiciled in different states. But noncitizens cannot.

2. Was the Missouri Compromise constitutional?

3. What was the effect of the transportation of Scott into nonslave states on his original status in Missouri?

The Supreme Court decided the case in 1857, a year in which the United States was profoundly split due to the issue of slavery. There can be no doubt that the Court attempted to take that issue "out of politics"—a point to which I will return.

Was Dred Scott a Citizen?

Justice Taney's opinion held first that Scott was not a citizen of Missouri. Therefore the federal courts had no jurisdiction over the case.

This was a complex issue. There is no definition of the term "citizen" for purposes of diversity jurisdiction. Perhaps we should say that Scott's status as a citizen of Missouri depends on Missouri law, and perhaps the question whether Scott is a citizen of Missouri depends on whether Scott was still a slave. No one disputed that slaves do not qualify as citizens.

But Justice Taney went very much further than this. He did not rely on Missouri law, but argued very broadly that *no person descended from an American slave could ever be a citizen for constitutional purposes.* Under the Constitution, "they are not included . . . under the word citizen and can therefore claim none of the rights and privileges of citizens." It is here that Taney could not rely on constitutional text, which was ambiguous, but resorted explicitly and self-consciously to an understanding of original intentions. Thus he wrote: "On the contrary, [descendants of Africans] were at that time considered as a subordinate and inferior class of beings, who had been subjugated by the dominant race, and whether emancipated or not, yet remained subject to their authority, and had no rights or privileges but such as those who held the power and the Government might choose to grant them."

As already noted, this was one of the first self-consciously "originalist" opinions of the Supreme Court. On this issue, the Court spoke for its understanding of what the framers believed. (We cannot indict a method on the ground that it has been misapplied; but it is worth noting that the Court was attempting to speak for history and couched its decision explicitly in historical terms.)

Was the Missouri Compromise Constitutional?

At first glance, the Court's jurisdictional conclusion should have been the end of the matter. If Scott was not a citizen of Missouri,

71

the federal courts had no authority to hear his complaint, and the case should have ended, at least for Chief Justice Taney.

But the Court went on to consider the huge question of whether Scott remained a slave after living in Illinois and the Louisiana Territory. The Court said that he did. But why? This question is much harder to answer.

Perhaps it was Missouri law that governed the issue of whether Scott, a resident there, was still a slave in another state. Four justices so concluded. This idea is not implausible, and for those justices there was no reason to speak to the constitutional validity of the Missouri Compromise. But three of them did so anyhow. Thus a total of six justices concluded that Scott was still a slave because the Missouri Compromise was unconstitutional. Why was this so?

Chief Justice Taney offered several arguments. First, he said that Congress's authority to "make all needful Rules and Regulations respecting the Territory or other Property belonging to the United States" did not extend to territories not owned in 1789. By itself this should have been sufficient, but perhaps it did not seem plausible even to Chief Justice Taney, so he offered a second point: he said that slavery was constitutionally sacrosanct, so that even if Congress had authority over new territories, it could not ban slavery there. "[T]he right of property in a slave is distinctly and expressly affirmed in the Constitution." But this too was an adventurous conclusion. Thus Justice Taney added a third point, to the effect that Congress's power over the territories could not collide with other constitutional limitations. Congress could not, for example, eliminate freedom of speech in the territories. And this point was decisive for the question at hand. A law that deprives someone of property because he has brought it into a particular place "could hardly be dignified with the name of due process of law."

This was an exceptionally important moment in American law. It was the birthplace of the idea of "substantive due process," the idea used in the *Lochner*-era cases, in *Roe v. Wade*, and in many of the most controversial decisions in the Court's history.

Why was this a new idea? On its face, the due process clause appears to give people a right to a hearing to contest factual findings, and Sandford sought much more than that. Does the due process clause give courts authority to strike down legislation as unreasonable or as substantively unjust? Before *Dred Scott*, the Supreme Court had not suggested that it did. The suggestion was textually awkward, to say the least. The due process clause seems to speak of procedure, not of substance.

Even if the due process clause is understood to have a substantive dimension, there is a big problem with the Court's argument. International law had long held that a master who voluntarily takes a slave into free territory thereby relinquishes his property interest in the slave. So long as the territory is known to be a free one, this is not a "taking" of property. If California says that people may not own lions, and if a citizen from Arizona takes a lion into California, there is no constitutional problem if the lion is taken from the owner and even freed in California. Even with Justice Taney's assumptions, his argument was remarkably brisk and unconvincing. I return to this point below.

The Effect of Interstate Transport

It might appear at this point that the Court had a narrow route to resolution of the case. Perhaps a free slave could be deemed a citizen for purposes of jurisdiction. Perhaps the Court need not have assessed the constitutionality of the Missouri Compromise. And perhaps the crucial issue in the case was whether Missouri had to recognize any change in Scott's status as a result of his visit into free areas. If Missouri did not have to recognize that change, the case was over. And if Scott's stay in Illinois produced a change in status that Missouri had to respect, the case was over as well.

In fact, the justices initially concluded that they would not decide the largest issues in the case and that they would conclude very simply that, under Missouri law, Scott was still a slave. If that was so, the case could be resolved simply and without broad pronouncements. But shortly after his election, President James Buchanan wrote to one of the justices suggesting that it was important "to destroy the dangerous slavery agitation and thus restore peace to our distracted country." A variety of factors thus moved Justice James Wayne to insist that the Court should deal with the two key issues—the status of the Missouri Compromise and the status of freed blacks as citizens—on which the justices originally decided to remain silent. Five justices eventually agreed; all were from slave states.

Justice Wayne later told a Southern senator that he had "gained a triumph for the Southern section of the country, by persuading the chief justice that the court could put an end to all further agitation on the subject of slavery in the territories." Here is the obvious punch line: for palpable political reasons, the Court was persuaded to speak to all of the key questions. Its obvious goal was to solve, for all time, the great moral and political crisis that slavery had created for the United States of America.

Dred Scott: Judicial Hubris

Now we are in a position to explore the question: What was wrong with the *Dred Scott* opinion? Let us divide potential answers into two categories: institutional and substantive. The substantive answers have to do with the best reading of the Constitution. The institutional answers have to do with the appropriate role of the Supreme Court in American government. The two are related, but it is both useful and important to try to separate them.

Begin with issues of substance. The Court was not just reckless but simply wrong to say what it did with respect to the status of freed slaves. There was no basis for the Court's conclusion that freed slaves could not count as citizens. In fact, some freed slaves participated in the ratification of the Constititution itself; and freed slaves were allowed to vote in at least five of the colonies. The Constitution does not suggest that free citizens do not stand on the same ground as everybody else.

In fact, the text of the Constitution—its infamous "three-fifths clause"—itself undermines the Court's conclusion. If slaves count for three-fifths of a human being for the apportioning of representatives (a provision that recognizes without endorsing slavery, and that itself creates an incentive to eliminate slavery), then freed slaves count as 100 percent human beings for these same purposes. Hence the Constitution expressly distinguishes not between African and non-African descendants, but between slaves and free persons, whether African or not. This part of the constitutional text was not mentioned in *Dred Scott*, but it argues strongly the other way.

More generally, the Constitution does nothing to entrench slavery. It recognizes the existence of the institution but does little more than that.[6] Certainly some of the Constitution's framers believed that slavery was acceptable or desirable (though consider slaveholder Thomas Jefferson's suggestion that "I tremble for my country" when contemplating that God is just). Maybe a majority of them thought so. But they did not put that judgment in the Constitution itself. There was no reason to think that freed slaves should not qualify as citizens for constitutional purposes.

The Court's decision with respect to the Missouri Compromise was also both reckless and wrong. On its face, congressional power over the territories is extremely broad. It is absurd to say that this power was limited to existing territories. To be sure, this power cannot be used to violate the Constitution itself; Congress could not outlaw political dissent within the territories. On this score, the *Dred Scott* Court was correct. But contrary to the Court's suggestion, the Constitution does not distinctly and expressly affirm the property rights of slave owners. It recognizes, somewhat obliquely, the institution of slavery, but it does not endorse that institution. Indeed, it forbids Congress from outlawing the slave trade only until 1808, a provision that is hardly a ringing endorsement of the institution of slavery. And as I have said, the use of substantive due process—even if there is such a thing—was unsupportable because there is no "taking" of property when one state gives notice that certain goods (guns, bombs) are not allowed there.

So much for constitutional substance. I think the institutional issues are more important, more subtle, and of more enduring relevance. There are two points here.

First, the Court reached out to answer numerous questions not requiring a judicial answer in the case at hand. Once it found that

Scott was not a citizen, the case was at an end. The Court lacked jurisdiction. Or it could have said very modestly, and without pronouncing on the Missouri Compromise or the citizenship question, that Missouri law controlled Scott's status as a citizen in Missouri. There are good reasons for the old idea that courts should decide only those issues necessary to the resolution of the case at hand. This idea minimizes the role of judges in the constitutional regime and allows room for democratic deliberation and debate. Amazingly, the *Dred Scott* Court took the opposite approach; it decided *every* issue raised by the case, regardless of whether the decision was necessary to settle Scott's complaint.

Second and foremost, the nation was in the midst of an extraordinary, deep, and wide debate about one of the central moral issues of the time. It is ludicrous to suppose that nine lawyers in Washington could lay this issue to rest by appeal to the Constitution. It is hubristic for nine lawyers charged with interpreting the Constitution to think they know the right answer for the nation as a whole. In such cases the likelihood of error is very high, and the likelihood of success—a final resolution for a heterogeneous nation—is low even if there is no error. The Court should have proceeded with great caution unless it found the Constitution unambiguous on the point or unless it thought the moral principle so urgent and so plausibly constitutional in character that it required judicial endorsement. Neither of these could be said for *Dred Scott*. The Court should have decided the case narrowly by asking about the status of Missouri law.

LINCOLN AND JUDICIAL INSTITUTIONS

I want to say a word now about the nation's reaction to *Dred Scott*, and about the appropriate response of citizens and public officials to Supreme Court decisions. My basic point is this: the Supreme Court has the last word on cases it decides. But interpretation of the Constitution is emphatically not only a judicial activity. Constitutional interpretation is for others as well. The Supreme Court is supreme, but only in a limited way. It does not preclude constitutional complaints by others seeking change. Certainly this is so when issues of constitutional law are also issues of basic political principle. In such cases it is especially important to insist—as have Presidents Jefferson, Franklin Roosevelt, and Ronald Reagan, among others—that the Supreme Court has no monopoly on constitutional interpretation.

Consider, in this regard, Abraham Lincoln's words: "If this important decision had been made by the unanimous concurrence of the judges, and without any apparent partisan bias and in accordance with legal public expectation, and with the steady practice of the departments throughout our history, and had been in no part, based on assumed historical facts, which are not really true or, if wanting in some of these, had been affirmed and reaffirmed, it might be factious, even revolutionary, to not acquiesce in it. But when we find it wanting in all these claims to public confidence, it is not resistance, it is not factious, it is not even disrespectful, to treat it as not having yet quite established a settled doctrine for the country." And in 1858 Lincoln said: "If I were in Congress and a vote should come up on a question whether slavery should be prohibited in a new territory, in spite of that *Dred Scott* decision, I would vote that it should."

Lincoln's simplest and most dramatic statement on the topic, made in his First Inaugural Address, echoed the theme of democratic deliberation and a shared role in constitutional interpretation: "The candid citizen must confess that if the policy of the government, upon vital questions affecting the whole people, is to be irrevocably fixed by decisions of the Supreme Court, the instant they are made, in ordinary litigation between parties in personal actions, the people will have ceased to be their own rulers, having to that extent practically resigned the government into the hands of that eminent tribunal."

In this light we might see the Court as having a dialogic relation with others engaged in political and moral deliberation, and with others who are thinking about the meaning of the Constitution. The *Dred Scott* Court fostered no such dialogue. In fact, its whole goal was preclusive. But it is predictable in such circumstances that the Court will fail and that voices will be loudly raised against it. This is certainly so for the most invasive decisions in the Court's history—*Dred Scott, Lochner v. New York, Roe v. Wade, Buckley v. Valeo*. What the Court ought to do, generally and to the extent that it can, is to act as a participant in democratic deliberation, not as the unique "forum of principle" in American government.

Needless to say, this is an argument for a degree of judicial statesmanship.[7] It is an argument that there is no mechanism to determine the Constitution's meaning; that meaning is a function of judgment; and that judgment, rightly exercised, involves both substantive issues and institutional constraints.

Lessons Drawn and Applied: Affirmative Action, Homosexuality, the Right to Die

In General

I have said that *Dred Scott* was a blunder and an abuse because it purported to resolve many more issues than were before the Court, and in that way attempted to resolve issues of high principle that are fundamentally of a public, not a judicial, nature. Let us take *Dred Scott* to suggest the following points. First, courts should generally not set forth broad theories of the good or the right; they should try to bracket those issues and leave them for other places. Second, they should, to the extent possible and in general, decide cases by reference to modest, low-level rationales on which diverse people can agree.

We might say that in constitutional cases, courts should adopt *incompletely theorized agreements*, and in that way economize on moral disagreement. This is perfectly familiar in ordinary life—in families, workplaces, and elsewhere. We can imagine many settings in which people who disagree on large abstractions can agree on particular cases. Certainly this fact is often true for a faculty; it is true, too, for a polity. In doing this, courts can lower the costs of decision and also the costs of error. And they can accomplish one of the most important goals of a well-functioning deliberative democracy: promote necessary agreement while minimizing the problems created by fundamental disagreement.

Judicial casuistry has another feature. When they are in the midst of a political thicket, courts should not decide more cases than have been placed before them. That is, they should, generally and to the extent possible, decide cases with close reference to the particular issues presented. This strategy decreases the cost of decision, and decreased costs are a significant gain. This strategy also allows large scope for democratic self-governance. It does this because it can trigger public debate and signal the existence of issues of high principle without foreclosing fresh thinking or disallowing the democratic public from resolving the foundational issues as it chooses.

Affirmative Action

Now let us try to apply these thoughts to some contemporary issues. The nation is in the midst of a large debate over color-conscious programs, and many people have vigorously urged the Supreme Court to foreclose such programs, whether deemed "affirmative action" or something else. There are passages in Supreme Court decisions that read roughly like this: "In the Civil War, the nation decided on a principle of color-blindness. Whether this is a desirable or wise principle is not for us to say. But the issue has been foreclosed by our heritage."

Or it might be said, as a court of appeals recently did, that the equal protection clause has come to be understood to embody a principle of race neutrality that is violated by all affirmative action programs, including those in the educational system. Thus, in its remarkable decision striking down an affirmative action plan for the University of Texas Law School, the court of appeals said that race-consciousness was acceptable only to remedy identified acts of past discrimination. Thus public universities must proceed on a race-neutral basis. (Through statutory law, this view may extend to private universities as well.)

In this form, a court opinion outlawing affirmative action is closely analogous to *Dred Scott*, and defective—abusive, overreaching—for the same reason. It would be an amazing act of hubris. In one form, a supposed past historical judgment, itself not clearly embodied in the constitutional text,[8] is used to foreclose democratic experimentation. (Recall *Dred Scott* on citizenship and the Missouri Compromise.) In another form, a general principle ("color-blindness") is announced to foreclose such experimentation even though the principle covers a wide range of situations, some of which seem to draw the principle in some doubt (as where race is a minor factor used alongside many other minor factors). We might compare the narrower, fact-intensive, casuistical approaches characteristic of Justice Lewis Powell Jr. in the Bakke case and, on occasion, of Justice Sandra Day O'Connor.

My simple proposition is this: there are many kinds of affirmative action programs. The nation has embarked on a large-scale debate about such programs. That debate raises issues of both morality and fact. Ultimately the place of affirmative action programs should be decided democratically, not judicially. There is no sufficiently clear constitutional commitment to color blindness to justify judicial intrusion.

Of course this is not to say that affirmative action programs are always good. Some of them are very bad. In any case, they are extraordinarily diverse. Their validity depends on the details, and in these circumstances, courts should be attentive to the details. They should proceed modestly and casuistically.

We are now in a position to discuss the possible catalytic role of the Supreme Court insofar as that role bears on the affirmative action debate. Suppose that it is agreed that the issue of affirmative action should be decided democratically rather than judicially—but suppose, too, that institutions are operating in such a way as to ensure that many public decisions are taken in an unaccountable way and are not really a product of democratic judgments. This is a plausible description of affirmative action programs of the period, say, 1975 to 1990. A meandering, casuistical, rule-free path may well be a salutary way of signaling the existence of large questions of policy and principle, at least with constitutional dimensions, when those questions would otherwise receive far less attention than they deserve. Hence the participants in Supreme Court cases have become familiar "characters" in the national debate, helping to frame discussion: Bakke, Weber, Johnson, minority construction contractors, and others.

In fact, the Court has mostly acted in this way. Some of the justices have undoubtedly been aware of the difficulty and variousness of the affirmative action problem and have chosen a casuistical approach for this reason. The Court's decisions have been among the factors that have kept affirmative action in the public eye and helped focus the public on issues of principle and policy. This is the best that can be said for the Court's rule-free path. When it confronts admissions policies like that of the University of Texas, the Court should continue in this way, looking closely at the details and avoiding broad pronouncements. It would be a democratic disaster if the Court, *Dred Scott*-style, were to foreclose further democratic debate in the name of the "color-blindness" principle.

The Right to Die

The right-to-die debate is along one dimension significantly different from the debate over affirmative action. Here the relevant laws have been on the books for a long time, and they have not, as a general rule, been revisited by recently elected officials.

Do such laws invade a constitutional "right to privacy"? Many people and some courts think so. Invoking the authority of *Roe v. Wade*, such people say that the government cannot legitimately interfere with self-regarding choices about what to do "with their bodies," and that therefore the choice is for the individual, not for the state. Several courts have recently gone in this direction.

Thus stated, the argument for a constitutional right to die raises many questions and many doubts. Substantive due process does not deserve wide acceptance. For reasons I have suggested, it is textually awkward, to say the least. Moreover, the conditions in which a right to die might be asserted are widely variable. Perhaps some people choosing death would be confused or myopic. Perhaps some doctors would overbear their patients; perhaps some families could not entirely be trusted. In view of the complexity of the underlying issues of value and fact—our now-familiar theme—courts should be extremely reluctant to try to resolve this issue through judicial declaration. They lack the fact-finding expertise and policymaking competence. Thus recent court decisions announcing a large-scale "right to die" are another version of the *Hopwood* case; they are modest reruns of *Dred Scott* itself.

Does this mean that courts should say nothing at all? Perhaps. But there is an alternative, and it bears on the principal difference between the affirmative action controversy and the controversy over the right to die. I think that a promising and ingenious solution, set out by Judge Guido Calabresi, attempts to promote a kind of dialogue between courts and the public. Let us notice first that the relevant laws were enacted long ago. They were designed to prevent people from being accessories to suicide; that was their fundamental purpose. Suicide was considered a genuine crime. But this reason for the statutes no longer holds much weight. Enforcement of those laws has fallen into near desuetude. In any case, these are not ordinary cases of suicide, and the technology has much changed, making possible forms of euthanasia that would have been unimaginable when the laws were first enacted.

The central point, for those interested in democratic deliberation, is that in some states there has been no recent engagement with the underlying moral and technological issues. In these circumstances, it is appropriate for a court to say that the state has not demonstrated an adequate reason to interfere with a private choice of this kind—unless and until a recent legislature is able to show that there is a sufficiently recent commitment to this effect to support fresh legislation.

Understood in this way, the right to die cases are reminiscent of the Connecticut contraceptives case, *Griswold v. Connecticut*, as I would understand that case in the light of *Dred Scott*. In *Griswold*, the Court embarked on the task of taking large-scale positions on matters of political morality by speaking of a nonexistent constitutional "right of privacy." Instead, the Court might have taken a very narrow approach in *Griswold*. It might have said that laws that lack real enforcement, that appear no longer to reflect considered political convictions, cannot be used against private citizens in decisions of this kind on what is predictably and almost inevitably a random basis.

The underlying, time-honored principle—that involving desuetude—has strong democratic foundations. The principle condemning desuetude says that when an old law is practically unenforced because it does not receive sufficient public approval, ordinary citizens are permitted to violate it, and in that way to call democratic attention to the space between the law as popularly conceived and approved and the law as it exists on the books.

An idea of this sort, I suggest, would be a singularly good way of beginning the constitutional debate about the right to die. It would not involve judicial prohibition. It would begin the debate by putting the burden of deliberation on representative bodies accountable to the people.

Homosexuality

Now turn to claims that the Constitution forbids discrimination on the basis of sexual orientation. Here plaintiffs' lawyers are invoking a principle of human equality to invalidate democratic outcomes. Here some people insist that a properly capacious notion of constitutional equality adequately justifies an aggressive judicial role.

I will assert, without defending the point here, that that notion of equality does seem to me to connect very well with the equality principle that underlies the Civil War amendments. Let us simply assume that this claim is right. We might even assume, at least for purposes of argument, that the rightness of the constitutional claim is very clear, and that the homosexual case is therefore different from cases involving affirmative action and the right to die, which seem in any case difficult. And then—having made things especially hard for ourselves—let us ask about the Court's appropriate role, returning to Abraham Lincoln in the process.

Abraham Lincoln always insisted that slavery was wrong. On the basic principle, Lincoln allowed no compromises; no justification was available for chattel slavery. But on the question of means, Lincoln was quite equivocal—flexible, strategic, open to compromise, aware of doubt. The fact that slavery was wrong did not mean that it had to be eliminated immediately, or that blacks and whites had to be placed immediately on a plane of equality. In Lincoln's view, the feeling of "the great mass of white people" would not permit this result, as is evident in his most striking formulation: "Whether this feeling accords with justice and sound argument, is not the sole question, if indeed, it is any part of it. A universal feeling, whether well or ill-founded, can not be safely disregarded." What is most notable about this claim is the view that the inconsistency of a "feeling" with justice or sound argument may be *irrelevant* to the question of what to do at any particular point in time.

In Lincoln's view, efforts to create immediate social change in this especially sensitive area could have disastrous unintended consequences or could backfire, even if those efforts were founded on entirely sound principles. It was necessary first to educate people about the reasons for the change. Important interests had to be accommodated or persuaded to come on board. Issues of timing were crucial. Critics had to be heard and respected. For Lincoln, rigidity about the principle would always be combined with caution about the means by which the just outcome would be brought about. For this reason, it is a mistake to see Lincoln's caution with respect to abolition as indicating uncertainty about the underlying principle. But it is equally mistaken to think that Lincoln's certainty about the principle entailed immediate implementation of racial equality.

The point is highly relevant to constitutional law, especially in the area of social reform. To return to my basic theme: as it operates in the courts, constitutional law is a peculiar mixture of substantive theory and institutional constraint. Suppose, for example, that the ban on same-sex marriage is challenged on equal protection grounds. Even if judges find the challenge plausible in substance, there is much reason for caution on the part of the courts. An immediate judicial vindication of the principle could well jeopardize important interests. It could galvanize opposition. It could weaken the antidiscrimination movement itself as that movement is operating in democratic arenas (compare *Roe v.*

Wade). It could provoke more hostility and even violence against homosexuals. It would certainly jeopardize the authority of the judiciary.

Is it too pragmatic and strategic, too obtusely unprincipled, to suggest that judges should take account of these considerations? I do not believe so. Prudence is not the only virtue; it is certainly not the master virtue, but it is a virtue nonetheless. At a minimum, it seems plausible to suggest that courts should generally use their discretion over their docket in order to limit the timing of relevant intrusions into the political process. It also seems plausible to suggest that courts should be reluctant to vindicate even good principles when the vindication would compromise other interests, at least if those interests include, ultimately, the principles themselves.

In the area of homosexuality, we might make some distinctions. If the Supreme Court of the United States had accepted the view that states must authorize same-sex marriages in 1996, or even 1998, we should have expected a constitutional crisis, a weakening of the legitimacy of the Court, an intensifying hatred of homosexuals, a constitutional amendment overturning the Court's decision, and much more. Any Court should hesitate in the face of such prospects. It would be far better for the Court to do nothing—or better yet, to start cautiously and to proceed incrementally.

The Court might, for example, conclude that the equal protection clause forbids state constitutional amendments that forbid ordinary democratic processes to outlaw discrimination on the basis of sexual orientation. The Court might say that such amendments, of the sort that has been enacted (and invalidated judicially) in Colorado, do not merely discriminate on the basis of sexual orientation, but also disfavor a defined group in the political process, in a way that involves issues of both animus and political equality. A judicial ruling of this kind would be quite narrow. In fact, the Court proceeded very much in this way in its laudable decision in *Romer v. Evans*.

Or the Court might say—as some lower courts have done—that government cannot rationally discriminate against people of homosexual orientation without showing that those people have engaged in acts that harm some legitimate government interest. Narrow rulings of this sort would allow room for public discussion and debate before obtaining a centralized national ruling that preempts ordinary political process.

Armed with an understanding of *Dred Scott*, we can go much further. Constitutional law is not only for the courts; it is for all public officials. The original understanding was that deliberation about the Constitution's meaning would be part of the function of the president and legislators as well. The post-Warren Court identification of the Constitution with the decisions of the Supreme Court has badly disserved the traditional American commitment to deliberative democracy. In that system, all officials—not only the judges—have a duty of fidelity to the founding document. And in that system, we should expect that elected officials will have a degree of interpretive independence from the judiciar. We should even expect that they will sometimes fill the institutional gap created by the courts' lack of fact-finding ability and policymaking competence. For this reason, they may conclude that practices are unconstitutional even if the Court would uphold them, or that practices are valid even if the Court would invalidate them. Lincoln is an important example here as well. Often he invoked constitutional principles to challenge chattel slavery, even though the Supreme Court had rejected that reading of the Constitution in the Dred Scott case.

CONCLUSION

It is time to conclude. The *Dred Scott* opinion was an abomination, and it was an abomination in two different ways. The first has to do with substantive law: freed slaves should have qualified as citizens. The Missouri Compromise was a legitimate exercise of legislative authority. The serious question in the case was whether Missouri's view about Scott's status was binding. That was a little question, not a big one, and the Court should have stayed with the little question.

But *Dred Scott* was also an abomination in ways that have to do with institutional role. The Court did not merely decide Dred Scott's case; it managed at once to assert that it lacked jurisdiction and to strike down an act of Congress not directly bearing on the jurisdictional issue—an especially neat trick. The Court purported to make the original intentions of the framers binding, even though those intentions were murky, did not compel the Court's conclusion, and were not in the Constitution itself. Perhaps worst of all, the Court deliberately reached out to decide nationally crucial issues that deserved and would ultimately receive an answer from the people rather than the judiciary.

Thus understood, *Dred Scott* offers many lessons for those interested in the modern Supreme Court. As a general presumption, it argues against efforts to take the great moral issues out of politics. It argues in favor of an approach that sees constitutional interpretation and moral deliberation as tasks for representatives and citizens generally, not just for judges. It suggests that the great issues of political morality—affirmative action, the right to die, homosexual rights—are mostly for political processes, not for courts.

This does not suggest that courts should do nothing. I have argued that in all three areas, courts can perform a catalytic role. Democratic deliberation is not a mere matter of counting noses. The Court can do a great deal of good in promoting more rather than less in the way of both democracy and deliberation. It can do a great deal of bad in producing less rather than more of these things.

This, I suggest, is not a myth. It is the enduring lesson of *Dred Scott*. At least it is the enduring lesson for a Court that has an accommodating spirit, and that is not so sure that it is right.

CODA

I have a coda. It consists of notes about what happened to the people in the Scott case.

John Sanford was insane and institutionalized by the time the decision was announced. He died on May 5, 1857.

Despite the Court's decision, Dred Scott eventually won his freedom, because after the Court rendered its decision Irene Emerson and her new husband, Calvin Chaffee, took immediate measures to free Dred Scott. Scott lived as a free man—working as a hotel porter—for only a year before his death from tuberculosis in 1858.

Until very recently,[9] history had lost the stories of Harriet Scott, Eliza Scott, Lizzie Scott, and their descendants. We now know that Harriett Scott survived the Civil War and the Thirteenth Amendment; that Eliza never married and spent much of her life caring for her mother; that Lizzie had children and her great-grandson—Dred and Harriett's great-great grandson—is now living in Missouri.

Dred Scott's grave went unmarked and unnoticed for many decades; but at the centennial of the *Dred Scott* case, in 1957, a granddaughter of Taylor Blow provided a granite headstone for his grave, and it can now be seen in Calvary Cemetery in St. Louis, Missouri.

President Lincoln signed the Emancipation Proclamation on January 1, 1863. The nation—We, the People—ratified the Fourteenth Amendment in 1868, overruling *Dred Scott* through democratic means, with its opening words, "All persons born or naturalized in the United States are citizens of the United States and of the State wherein they reside."

NOTES

1. For the sake of readability, I have minimized footnotes and citations throughout. Of course, the Constitution did not abolish slavery. In fact, it recognized the existence of the institution of slavery, but without endorsing or entrenching it. See below.

2. 60 US at 93, 405 (1857).

3. These two qualifications are important. See below.

4. I describe these ideas in more detail in Cass R. Sunstein, *Legal Reasoning and Political Conflict* (Oxford University Press, 1996).

5. I acknowledge that this is an unconventional view and I do not attempt to defend this belief here.

6. More particularly, there are three relevant provisions. (1) Article 1, Section 9, prevents Congress from prohibiting the slave trade until 1808. This is hardly an endorsement of slavery. It gives slave states a relatively short period in which to import slaves, and then lets Congress do as it wishes. (2) Article 4, Section 3, requires nonslave states to return fugitive slaves to their owners. This provision is extremely limited; it does not say anything about the obligations of states to respect slave owners who voluntarily come, with their slaves, into nonslave states. (3) The so-called three-fifths clause, Article 1, Section 2, says that representatives and direct taxes shall be apportioned by adding to the whole number of free persons "three fifths of all other persons." This provision is designed for purposes of allocating representatives and direct taxes. As such, it creates an incentive to free slaves by giving slave states more political power if they become nonslave states. It certainly does not reflect any judgments that slaves are just 3/5 of "people."

7. It is emphatically not an argument for Bork-style "originalism." See Sunstein, *Legal Reasoning and Political Conflict.*

8. There is no evidence that the equal protection clause was intended to stop affirmative action, and there is considerable evidence to the contrary. In fact, those who ratified the Fourteenth Amendment engaged in race-conscious remedial programs. It would be most refreshing if some of the originalist justices on the Court, who tend to oppose affirmative action on constitutional grounds, would invoke some historical support for their views (it is hard to find any) or would say that although they personally do not like affirmative action, history forbids them from invalidating it on constitutional grounds.

9. A valuable discussion is Lea VanderVelde and Sandhya Subramanian, "Mrs. Dred Scott," 106 Yale L.J. 1033 (1997).

CHAPTER FOUR

Politics and Judicial Responsibility:
Dred Scott v. Sandford

JAMES M. McPHERSON

Cass Sunstein has offered a stimulating and provocative interpretation of the lesson that the *Dred Scott* case might provide to the Supreme Court in our own time. He maintains that not only was the majority ruling in the *Dred Scott* case egregiously wrong in substance, but also—and more important—that the Taney court was guilty of a disastrous and arrogant hubris in its attempt to settle an explosive political issue by a ruling that went far beyond the issues actually necessary to decide the case. Sunstein applies the lesson of the *Dred Scott* case to three controversial and potentially explosive issues before the Court today. He argues for "a degree of judicial statesmanship" by which the Court should rule on these issues on the narrowest possible grounds that will not preclude incremental resolution of the questions by political means through "democratic reflection and debate."

At first reading, Sunstein's argument struck me as a plausible and persuasive appeal for judicial minimalism. But on reflection I began to have some reservations. Since my own expertise is not in constitutional interpretation, I will leave the finer points of constitutional theory, especially as they apply to contemporary issues, to others. As a historian of the Civil War era, I will confine my remarks to the impact of the *Dred Scott* case in its own time.

First, I fully agree with Sunstein's substantive demolition of the majority ruling in the *Dred Scott* case. I believe that nearly all modern constitutional historians would agree with him. But let me enter one minor quibble. The chapter focuses on the majority *decision* in the case written by Chief Justice Roger Taney. Some people may not realize that two justices, Benjamin Curtis and

John McLean, vigorously dissented from the majority ruling. Their dissents, especially that of Curtis, anticipated most of the modern criticisms of Taney's decision. Curtis pointed out that Taney's ruling concerning the noncitizenship of blacks was not only gratuitous but just plain wrong, historically and constitutionally. And Curtis also maintained that a law prohibiting the ownership of slaves in a given territory was *not* a taking of property, any more than a law in California against bringing lions into the state would be a taking—though the example is Sunstein's, not Curtis's.

But this is not my main point. Rather, I want to focus on what I take to be Sunstein's main point—that the *Dred Scott* decision was *preclusive* in purpose with a tendency, or intention, to foreclose or undermine "democratic deliberation and debate." I agree that one of the purposes of Taney's decision was to preclude further debate on the divisive issue of the legality of slavery in the territories. But the *effect* of this decision was quite the opposite of preclusive. Instead of foreclosing further debate through the democratic political process, the *Dred Scott* decision stimulated and structured an intensified debate. Sunstein sees this as an undesirable outcome, for by this invasive ruling—his word—the Court injected itself into a political issue it had no business trying to decide, and by so doing polarized the country and helped bring on a terrible war in which 620,000 men lost their lives.

I would argue, in reply, that the *Dred Scott* ruling did not really polarize the country any more than it was already polarized by the issue of slavery in the territories. It is quite possible that this issue could not have been settled peacefully, either by the Court or by the political process. Ever since the introduction of the Wilmot Proviso in 1846, indeed in some ways ever since the Missouri Compromise in 1820, this issue had the potential to split the country. It had almost provoked the secession of several Southern states in 1850 before being temporarily papered over by the Compromise of 1850, which among other things left it up to the residents of New Mexico and Utah territories whether they wanted slavery. The Kansas-Nebraska Act of 1854 applied the same principle to those territories. That led to a literal civil war in Kansas territory.

Most Americans at the time *wanted* the Supreme Court to help resolve this issue—though they disagreed on what the resolution should be. That is why Congress included provisions in both the Compromise of 1850 and the Kansas-Nebraska Act for expedited appeal to the Supreme Court of any suit concerning slave property in the territories affected by these laws. Sooner or later, therefore, even if the Court had ducked the territorial question in the *Dred Scott* case, as Sunstein thinks it should have done, the Court probably would have been confronted with a similar question in another case. And waiting in the wings was *Lemmon v. the People*, a case in New York concerning the right of slave owners to be protected in their property rights when they brought their slaves into a free *state*—an issue, of course, that was also part of the Dred Scott case.

I agree with Sunstein—and with Abraham Lincoln—that "interpretation of the Constitution is emphatically not only a judicial activity." But perhaps the converse is also true—at least Americans in the 1850s believed it to be true: the Supreme Court cannot evade the political dimensions of its responsibilities. As one of the three branches of the federal government, the Court is an integral part of that government in its efforts to find solutions for the problems facing the country. That's why Congress expedited appeals to the Court in the Utah and New Mexico acts of 1850 and the Kansas-Nebraska Act of 1854.

In any event, the Court's ruling in the *Dred Scott* case became an integral part of the political debate after 1857. In 1858 Lincoln made the case the main focus of his efforts to define the Republican position and discredit the Democratic position on slavery in his famous debates with Stephen Douglas. So thoroughly did the Dred Scott decision pervade and structure the Lincoln-Douglas debates that in one of those debates a Douglas supporter shouted from the audience to Lincoln: "Give us something besides Dred Scott." Quick as a cat, Lincoln responded: "Yes; no doubt you want to hear something that don't hurt." It was in the debate at Freeport, Illinois, that Lincoln forced Douglas to enunciate—not for the first time—what became known as the Freeport Doctrine. By asking Douglas whether there was any lawful way that residents of a territory could exclude slavery, Lincoln compelled Douglas to highlight the contradiction between his own policy of popular sovereignty and the rejection of that concept by the Dred Scott decision, which, as a good Democrat, Douglas had said he supported. In his reply, Douglas tried to have it both ways: the Court's ruling, he acknowledged, gave slaveholders the legal right to bring their slaves into the territories, but the residents of a territory could make that a worthless right by failing to enact or enforce local protective legislation.

This straddle came back to haunt Douglas in 1860, when Southern Democrats split the party in two over their demand for a federal slave code to enforce the right of slavery in the territories—in other words, to enforce the *Dred Scott* decision. This Democratic schism ensured Lincoln's election. Without the *Dred Scott* decision, it is quite possible that Lincoln would never have become president of the United States.

A final thought. One of the purposes of Section 1 of the Fourteenth Amendment was to overturn the *Dred Scott* ruling denying citizenship to African-Americans. If it had not been for the *Dred Scott* decision, it is quite possible that the Fourteenth Amendment would have been less expansive and that the provisions concerning privileges and immunities, due process, and equal protection, which are the basis for most modern civil rights jurisprudence and legislation, would not have existed in the form they do. Perhaps the cause of equal rights owes more to Roger Taney than one might ever have imagined.

CHAPTER FIVE

Lochner v. New York and the
Cast of Our Laws

HADLEY ARKES

In a series already amply distinguished, I have received an assignment even more distinguished yet: I have been entrusted with the task of explaining the only case in this volume that has been converted into a verb. No one has ever threatened "to Marbury" or "to Dred Scott it," but as Robert Bork has observed, "to Lochnerize" has become a term of derision among people with an interest in constitutional law. Of course, Judge Bork ought to know, because his name too has been converted into a verb, and he has done Lochner one better: his name has become a transitive verb: "to Bork" a candidate to the Supreme Court is to conduct an orchestrated campaign against confirmation. But in Bork's estimate, the opinion in the Lochner case, written by Rufus Peckham, "lives in the law as a symbol, indeed the quintessence, of judicial usurpation of power. . . . To this day [says Bork], when a judge simply makes up the Constitution, he is said 'to Lochnerize,' usually by someone who does not like the result."[1]

For the historians, *Lochner* stands for the laissez-faire Court of the late nineteenth century, spilling over into the twentieth. It was, supposedly, a conservative Court, which brought to the cases a deep suspicion of legislators and their motives when they flexed their powers and sought to be overly inventive in regulating business. As I will try to show, there are ample grounds for doubting all of the ingredients in this caricature, including the conservatism of that Court. But for Bork, *Lochner* stands also for the evils of "substantive due process": it marks an activist judiciary that was not content to test any law by its formal properties but was altogether too willing to test, and challenge, the substance of the law itself. Justice Stanley Matthews had declared in the old Yick Wo case that the judges could not be confined to look merely at the forms and blind themselves to the substance of what was done.[2] And those who are not trained as lawyers would think there is an elementary sense of justice here: the judges could not be confined to the task of gauging whether a law has been passed in a formally correct way, or whether there have been ample procedures for the defendants. Daniel Webster set everything in place long ago, in a manner that should have foreclosed all of the anguish that would be expended in later years, by conservatives as well as liberals, over "substantive due process." In his argument in the Dartmouth College case in 1819, Webster took care to explain why the "due process of law" could not be satisfied simply by the report that a bill had been enacted into law by a legislature with a procedure properly fastidious and solemn:

> Every thing which may pass under the form of an enactment, is not ... to be considered the law of the land. If this were so, acts of attainder, bills of pains and penalities, acts of confiscation, acts reversing judgments, and acts directly transferring one man's estate to another, legislative judgments, decrees, and forfeitures, in all possible forms, would be the law of the land. Such a strange construction would render constitutional provisions of the highest importance completely inoperative and void. It would tend directly to establish the unions of all powers in the legislature.[3]

The founders recognized that there could in fact be unjust laws, legal enactments that lacked the substance of justice.[4] And if they understood that the judges would be obliged to test legislation against the principles of the Constitution, it is quite arguable that there had to be implicit, in that vocation, the possibility of judging the rightness, the arbitrariness, or the justification of what was enacted into law.

But Robert Bork reflected a perspective that doubted, at the core, that there could be any reasoned or dispassionate judgment about the arbitrariness, or the justification, of what a legislature would enact. If we go back for a moment to that line I cited earlier, Bork referred to judges who were willing to strike down legislation—or in effect "make up" the Constitution—because they did not "like" the result. Bork himself treats arguments quite seriously, but for many positivists the arguments simply dissolve into those gut reactions of "like" and "dislike." Judges such as Stephen Field or George Sutherland managed to marshal precise reasons, in a compelling way, but at the end of the day, the reason would be reduced to the translation provided by the positivists. They would merely signal the fact that Field or Sutherland did not "like" what the legislature had done. To speak of the things that were right or wrong, justified or unjustified, was really to speak of the things that we simply liked or disliked, or in Humean terms, the things that gave us pleasure or displeasure.

In that respect, the positivists offer a lingering reflection of Justice Hugo Black, Franklin Roosevelt's first appointment to the Supreme Court, and the most emphatic, the most unreconstructed, opponent of "substantive due" process. He was also, therefore, the most implacable opponent of natural law. And on that point, there was never a shade of doubt: behind substantive due process, there had to be some notion of natural law or natural right—some claim to have access to an objective truth, perhaps a truth grounded in nature, or a truth grounded in the law of reason. But whatever the source from which it sprung, it would be a truth that did not depend on the votes of a majority. For after all, if all truth were conventional, then the only measure of truth would be found in the votes of majorities. And in that case, the function of the judge could only be as Justice Oliver Wendell Holmes described it: to assure that the herd gets its way—that the majority be allowed to prevail in some decorous manner, with the trappings of legality. In one notable case in the 1920s, Holmes dissented and urged his colleagues to hold back their hand rather than interfere with the authority of a legislature to make laws regulating the economy. As Holmes put it, with his characteristic sharpness, "the legislature may forbid or restrict any business when it has a sufficient force of public opinion behind it."[5] That was, of course, positivism with a vengeance; and it was the voice that rejected, without a tremor of qualification, the jurisprudence of "substantive due process."

In our own day, Bork and William Rehnquist come closer than any other judges in sharing Hugo Black's perspective and his dubiety about "substantive due process," which is why it could be said, in a half-jest, that Rehnquist and Bork may be the last judges of the New Deal. Bork, we will remember, got himself into deep trouble because of the criticism he directed at *Griswold v. Connecticut*, with its new doctrines of "privacy." That was of course the case on contraception in 1965, and it would be the prelude, most notably, to *Roe v. Wade* in 1973. It could be said that with *Griswold*, in 1965, and *Roe v. Wade*, jurisprudence moved into a new register. For some people in the law schools, jurisprudence truly begins with *Griswold*: everything before Griswold is taken to be a reflection of another historic epoch, whose teachings, whose doctrines, bear no validity in this new epoch of our own day. Just a few years ago, in fact, the remark was reported to me from a young professor of law that *Griswold* and *Roe* are regarded as the new touchstones in our jurisprudence: any theory of the law that yields the "wrong" result in *Griswold* or *Roe* is marked instantly as suspect or invalid. Robert Bork failed in confirmation precisely because he was regarded as a fifth vote to overrule *Roe v. Wade*, and so it cannot involve the slightest overstatement to say that *Griswold* and *Roe* mark the core of liberal jurisprudence in our own time. Yet it should also be clear that there is the sharpest, most dramatic contrast between modern liberal jurisprudence and the liberal jurisprudence of the New Deal, the jurisprudence that defined itself most crisply in opposition to substantive due process—and *Lochner v. New York*.

The clearest marker here, of course, is Justice Black: he was a vigorous dissenter in the *Griswold* case. He was the most emphatic opponent of this jurisprudence of privacy for the reasons that ran back to his own reigning doctrine. Black would explain this doctrine in the most compressed form by quoting Holmes: "A state legislature can do whatever it sees fit to do unless it is restrained by some express prohibition of the Constitution of the United States or of the State."[6] For Black, there could not have been the slightest question that a legislature could act to protect unborn children, just as it could act to protect endangered animals who were not even human. Black certainly understood that the legal protections for the child in the womb had been anchored in the common law, long before this country had even brought forth the Constitution.[7] When Black gave an account of his jurisprudence, he defined himself most sharply by the cases he was rejecting, and first on the list, at all times, was *Lochner v. New York*.

It becomes clear, beyond cavilling, that nothing in the liberal jurisprudence of the New Deal could have brought forth, or sustained, the jurisprudence of *Griswold* and *Roe v. Wade*. In fact, the irony is that it was quite the opposite: the jurisprudence of *Roe v. Wade* depended on the jurisprudence of those so-called reactionary judges—James McReynolds, George Sutherland, Pierce Butler, Willis Van Devanter—the judges who had resisted Roosevelt and the New Deal in the 1930s. The clues should have been impossible to miss: the proponents of the "right to an abortion" found the ground of that right in the "right of privacy," which was established, in their construal, over four or five cases. The two leading cases in the series were *Meyer v. Nebraska* (1923)[8] and *Pierce v. Society of Sisters* (1925).[9] Both decisions were written by the cantankerous, anti-Semitic Justice McReynolds.

But this is not to say, of course, that McReynolds and Sutherland were bound to approve of "the right to an abortion." Nor does it suggest that an understanding of "natural rights" would entail, or even support, the right to abortion, or any of the other claims spun out of *Griswold v. Connecticut.* It is simply that the argument for abortion requires an appeal to what may be called at least the "logic of natural rights": it requires an appeal to an understanding of rights that does not depend on the positive law of the Constitution or on the opinions of the majority reflected in legislatures.

But when we speak of the logic of natural rights, or the willingness to go beyond matters of procedure and test the substance of what legislatures enact into law, we are backing once again into the logic of "substantive due process." That is exactly what Justice Black had marshalled all his energies to oppose, and whenever he gave an account of the villainies he was resisting, in substantive due process, the case that headed the list was *Lochner v. New York.*

The last time he ran through the litany of cases for his audience, and denounced *Lochner v. New York,* was at the time his jurisprudence seemed to be at its height. It was 1963, he had just been celebrated the previous year for his twenty-fifth anniversary on the Court, and he could now speak for a unanimous Court in *Ferguson v. Skrupa.*[10] In that case, the state of Kansas had passed a law to restrict those people who made their living as "debt adjusters," in helping people to collect and arrange their debts. For some reason, which would probably raise our suspicions, the legislature had come to the judgment that only people with law degrees could engage in this occupation without imperiling the public safety. In the old Court, at the end of the nineteenth century, or in the Court of our own day, the judges would have looked at this legislation quite severely. But for Justice Black, the signs of arbitrariness were not to enter into the notice of the judges. We are no more in those dark times, as he said, when judges would presume to challenge the decisions made by representatives of the people. There would be no more inclination, he said, to strike down acts of legislation because judges "thought them unreasonable, that is, unwise or incompatible with some particular economic or social philosophy."[11]

This was the high tide of Justice Black's jurisprudence, in 1963, only two years before *Griswold* would turn jurisprudence on a different axis and Black would be left in disbelief. But he had with him, in 1962, a young acolyte in the newly appointed Justice Byron White. Years later, in 1977, White would invoke the memory of Hugo Black for the sake of showing just how much the world had turned between 1963 and 1977. The case was called *Moore v. East Cleveland,*[12] and I offer it here for the sake of highlighting, as White sought to highlight, the dramatic change in structure that had now been absorbed, settled. The case was hardly momentous, but it made it all the more remarkable that the Court was willing to take in, so readily, a case of this kind. The suburb of East Cleveland had an ordinance that sought to confine households to families, or it sought to avoid the complications brought by gatherings, perhaps even make-shift communes, with a cluster of unrelated people inhabiting the same house. But as the law was applied in this case, it threatened to punish a grandmother who had, within her household, two of her grandchildren who were cousins, but not siblings. (One grandson had come to live with her after his mother had died.) This gathering did not describe a "family" as it was defined under the local ordinance at the time. The Court had no trouble in judging the ordinance to be invalid; the statute imposed an arbitrary restriction on the freedom of this family to engage in some of the elementary decencies that one might expect of families. Still, Chief Justice Warren Burger thought that there had been no need for the Court to take the case: there had been no appeal to local authorities under the local procedures for appeal, and Burger registered his doubts that any sensible officials at the local level would really have insisted on applying this law, with its full stringency, to a case of this kind. But as to the substance of the judgment—or the fitness of this case to be reviewed by the federal courts—there was not a tremor of doubt.

The deeper doubt was registered by Justice White, who recorded his dissent mainly out of an interest in raising again the flag of the New Deal and of Justice Black. He reminded his colleagues that Black would have been astonished, if not rendered apoplectic, by a decision of this kind. White did not seem to doubt that the local ordinance reached too far, with a hand too heavy, and that it might even have been irrational. But as he recalled to his colleagues, Black had "never embraced the idea that the Due Process Clause empowered the courts to strike down merely unreasonable or arbitrary lgislation."[13] So long as an ordinance abridged nothing that was mentioned explicitly in the Constitution, Black would have been willing to sustain it. Apparently, White was willing to flag this case, and this moment, for the sake of conveying the lesson here more sharply: and the lesson was that we had now entered, quite emphatically, perhaps irreversibly, a different phase of our jurisprudence, with a radically different governing doctrine. Between 1963 and 1977, the jurisprudence of the New Deal had clearly been displaced and discredited. Along the way was *Roe v. Wade*, and of course, White, with a lingering attachment to Black, had been one of the two dissenters in the case. But if Black had been repudiated, along with the jurisprudence of the New Deal, it should be clear, beyond argument, that what was being repudiated now was the rejection of substantive due process. To put it another way, in repudiating Black, the Court in effect had to be installing a new a respect for all of those cases that Black himself had repudiated. He had repudiated, most pointedly, *Meyer v. Nebraska* and *Pierce v. Society of Sisters* on the authority of the family, but again, at the head of the list, as the leading case in the inventory, was *Lochner v. New York*.

Now, I have approached my problem through this indirect path, or through this odd angle, for reasons you may have already guessed. Without touching as yet on anything in the substance of *Lochner v. New York*, we may nevertheless reveal a deeper truth about *Lochner* that runs quite beyond the distractions cast up by the case, as we react to the facts that composed it. It is quite possible that, for reasons that are notably less than fundamental, we may be inclined to reach a different judgment in weighing the claims of the parties than the judgment struck off by the Court in that case in 1905. But our judgment may not dislodge the deeper premises or principles on which that decision was founded. And that point is brought home to us by this preliminary glimpse of *Lochner* threading through the memories and jurisprudence of a later day. Let us suppose for a moment that Justice Black and Judge Bork had it right: that *Lochner* stood for the tradition set against the jurisprudence of the New Deal. The deeper truth, then, that does not easily speak its name is that today we live firmly within the cast of *Lochner*. That case is ridiculed, derided, by the right as well as the left, and yet the structure of jurisprudence marked by the case is the structure that our judges, left and right, choose again, choose anew, whenever they are faced with the need to choose. *Lochner v. New York* is our law; it marks the juris-

101

prudence of our own day, even for people who profess to disagree with its result and who may even fancy that they are rejecting it at its root.

Perhaps the analogy here is the one I have drawn in other cases to the problem of the Republican leaders who drafted the Fourteenth Amendment. Senator Lyman Trumbull, a leader of the Republicans in the Senate, sought to assure his colleagues on one occasion that nothing in the Fourteenth Amendment would dislodge the laws in his own state of Illinois, or the laws in other states, that barred marriage across racial lines. As he argued to his colleagues, those laws on miscegenation were still compatible with the Fourteenth Amendment and the Equal Protection Clause because those laws bore equally on whites as well as blacks: they barred white people from marrying blacks, as they barred blacks from marrying whites.[14] But in our own day, of course, we would take a strikingly different view of the matter, or we think we could read the principle in a more stringent way. We see a couple barred from marriage, and we would argue that this couple is treated differently from other couples only because of the race of the people who constitute this coupling. We would be inclined to think that Senator Trumbull had made a mistake in his reasoning, or that he had been incomplete in his moral reasoning. But I don't think we would be so quick to say that Trumbull brought to this problem a moral perspective, or a set of principles, wholly at odds with our own. Trumbull had helped to draft the Fourteenth Amendment, he had brought to a new explicitness or articulation the principles that we would come to absorb more deeply as our own. In fact, it might be argued that we made our way to a more stringent reading of this principle only after Trumbull helped to teach a new generation that this was indeed one of the defining principles of the American law.

And so, in the same way, I would suggest that we would probably all be attached to the principles that formed the groundwork of *Lochner v. New York* even if some of us happened to be less clear on how we would have come down, exactly, in the case that presented itself to the judges. But one way of illuminating that groundwork is to approach the case from this odd angle, which moves in part by looking at the curious, reductive things that people were inclined to say about the case as they sought to discredit it. If we simply corrected the caricature and restored an accurate sense of the case, its truer groundwork may come into view along with the facts.

The curiosity here is deepened by the awareness that many of the facts defining the case are remarkably sketchy. The case arose from Utica, New York, in 1899, and it involved a law of New York State that mandated a limit of ten hours in the working day, or rather, ten hours on the average day, in a working week that had to be limited to sixty hours. A section of the law applied these provisions distinctly to bakeries. But one question was whether it applied to bakers as a *labor law,* a law designed to protect vulnerable or ignorant workmen against the dominant power of employers. Or was it to be regarded as a species of regulations on health, designed to protect the safety or health of the bakers? As it turned out, that distinction would make a difference, and it might have been telling, in this respect, that the broader statute, containing this section on bakeries, was a major piece of legislation passed in 1897 and styled "The Labor Law." Joseph Lochner was the owner of a bakery, and he was charged, in a criminal proceeding, for a misdemeanor in violating one section of "The Labor Law," which read this way:

> No employee shall be required or permitted to work in a biscuit, bread or cake bakery or confectionery establishment more than sixty hours in any one week or more than ten hours in any one day, unless for the purpose of making a shorter work day on the last day of the week; nor more hours in any one week than will make an average of ten hours per day for the number of days during such week in which such employe shall work.

Lochner was arrested on December 21, 1899, on the complaint of one of his employees, and here is where the record falls into a maddening sketchiness, which is not relieved at any stage. The complaint was apparently not brought by some worker claiming that Lochner had coerced him, against his will, to work longer hours. A probing of the records in Utica finally unearths the names of the principals, and those simple facts help to establish some rather elementary things: the action was brought by one Frank Couverette, who complained that Lochner had permitted another employee, Aman Schmitter, to work additional hours, beyond the limit mandated in the law. For some of us looking on, it would make a notable difference as to whether the notion of "permitted" here was a fiction, or whether Lochner really was making a different arrangement with a worker who was genuinely willing to work additional hours for additional, or overtime, pay. But these kinds of details are not contained in the record of any court that heard this case, at any level. What we can say, from the briefs and records, was that Lochner was convicted, that he faced a fine of twenty dollars or twenty days in jail. He paid the fine—and then proceeded to violate the law again. He permitted yet another baker to work past the mandated hours. Lochner was convicted again, fined fifty dollars this time—but now, with his resistance setting in, he launched the series of appeals that would carry him all the way to the Supreme Court. Along the way, he would move through two levels of appellate courts in New York, with the law sustained in each case, but in each case with divided courts.[15]

Of Lochner himself we know little. A search in the newspapers of Utica turned up his obituary in 1939 and brought forth these details: he was an immigrant from Bavaria, born in 1862. He had come to Utica at the age of twenty, and had worked for eight years as a baker before he eventually established what was called, in the newspapers, a "bakeshop" of his own. This did not exactly sound like a large, corporate bakery, and it was managed by a man who had himself sprung from the class of bakers. We would also suspect that he was still clocking many hours working by the ovens himself, though we still do not know anything about the tenor of his relations with his employees. Again, it made a notable difference as to whether this was a case of protecting workers against a coercive employer, or whether the case involved an interference with a worker who might in fact have wished to work additional hours for overtime pay. Justice Rufus Peckham was credited by his colleagues at the bar as the most careful, fastidious student of the record, and Peckham seemed to think it was a case of the latter:

that the controversy here involved a third party who objected to the fact that another worker had been *permitted* to work overtime.

That understanding of the case became an important lever used by Peckham in his opinion, and yet that is precisely the construction that the unions, or the supporters of the bill, insisted upon as they framed this case for a trial. Lochner himself had argued that he was being charged here with two crimes rather than one: he was being charged with the offense of *compelling* his workers, and on the other hand, of merely *permitting* his workers to work. He argued that they were two quite different things, that he could not be charged at the same time with coercing and permitting. In fact, his argument was that the latter—permitting a worker to work—could not tenably be a crime, and to the extent that the law actually covered the act of "permitting," it reached too far. It forbade people to work additional hours, even of their own volition, even when the added work could serve their interests. In this argument, Justice O'Brien, in dissent in the Supreme Court of New York, thought Lochner made a persuasive point.[16] But for the supporters of the law this was not such a bizarre construction. If the law mandates a policy, there is a serious question of whether the law may be subverted through a series of private contracts. We have right now laws that forbid discriminations on the basis of race and religion in hiring. A major donor to a university may offer a private bequest and append, as a condition, that no blacks or Jews be hired; but the law could be rendered a nullity if it could be subverted in that way through private contracts. The supporters of the law knew what they were doing then when they insisted on testing the law with its fuller reach. Whatever the circumstances in the case, they wished to present to the courts the law in its completeness, which covered the possibility of *permitting*, and not merely coercing, workers to work additional hours. Justice Peckham could hardly be faulted then for construing the case as the plaintiffs would have had him construe it.

But that brings us back to Justice Rufus Peckham, and perhaps the key was there: looking back myself, reflecting on what I had read about this case over the years, it struck me that the characterization of the case was often tied in with the characterization of

105

Peckham. And the supreme caricaturist here, with no peer, was Justice Holmes. As a college student, I recall being dazzled, as most youngsters would be, by the flourish of Holmes's prose, by his feistiness and crisp putdowns. He was a master of aphorism, and he coined the aphorism that would always dog Peckham's opinion in *Lochner*. No line is quoted more often in commentaries on this case than Holmes's line that "the Fourteenth Amendment did not enact Mr. Herbert Spencer's Social Statics."[17] The further, telling comparison, is that this line is usually quoted without quoting anything from Peckham's opinion, or without setting this aphorism against the body of Peckham's argument.

On reading the case a bit later, in graduate school, I found myself embarrassed to have admired Holmes's terse aphorism, for that is all that he had offered. It became clearer to me then that an aphorism does not supply an argument, or show, in measured terms, where a careful argument had been deficient. Holmes had not met Peckham's argument; he had merely caricatured the argument, just as he had caricatured Peckham himself in a letter, in a line that became instantly one of my favorites. As I returned to this matter, after an interval of thirty-five years, I found that the line was now bound up in the legends I had helped myself to preserve. Thinking back to Peckham, Holmes recalled that he used to say of him that "his major premise was God damn it."[18] The silent implication was that, for Peckham, this premise had proved remarkably serviceable; that it explained, as we say in the social sciences, a "large portion of the variance." The caricatures may then explain the understandings that came to be woven about the case, even if the portrait did not exactly fit the person or the arguments.

As to the person, there is a bit of a mystery. Peckham came from an established, connected family in upstate New York. He was sprung from the same, old-line, conservative Democratic families that encompassed the Roosevelts in Dutchess County. Peckham's father had been on the supreme court of the state, and Peckham would succeed him there as he had succeeded him in his law firm. But he also had an older brother, Wheeler Hazard Peckham, who had cut a noticeable figure in the law. Both brothers had a rather

106

independent streak, and both had been involved in reform politics in New York. But the elder brother had taken an active role in prosecuting the Tweed Ring in New York City.

One odd offshoot of that experience came in 1894, when Grover Cleveland nominated Wheeler Peckham to the Supreme Court. As a result of Wheeler Peckham's abrasions in the politics of New York, he found himself in the most curious position: nominated by a Democratic president, he still did not have the support of the two Democratic senators of his own state. In a strange turn, he was then denied confirmation in the Senate. To make matters even stranger, President Cleveland, the next year, put up the younger brother for another vacancy. As far as anyone could see, the politics of the two Peckhams were the same but the personal chemistry was quite different, the two senators were consulted, and Rufus was confirmed.

The Library of Congress contains papers of the Peckham family, running back to 1837 and labeled as the papers of Rufus Peckham. But in this compilation almost every letter and bill refers to Wheeler. There is virtually nothing of Rufus except copies of some modest memorials rendered at his funeral in Albany in 1909. There was a certain sadness to this life: Peckham and his wife had two sons, and in one of those cruel turns of life, both children died before the parents. I do not know whether Peckham decided to guard his private life in the style of Henry James, but he left us, as I say, with one of the most elusive and mysterious records: a collection of Rufus Peckham Papers almost entirely purged of any personal papers, and barren of any illumination of the principal, whose life, after all, had inspired the assembling of the papers.

There may be, in that story, an indirect reflection on the jurisprudence that he would represent; but that jurisprudence would be quite at odds with the caricature offered by Holmes. If I can return for the moment to the characterization left by Holmes, the sense here was that the jurisprudence was drawn from Herbert Spencer, that it represented a pure form of laissez-faire, that Peckham was a cranky, conservative judge, dubious about social experiments or socialist schemes. In this portrait, in other words,

Peckham began with a deep skepticism, with the presumption that schemes regulating business, or abridging the rights of property, were schemes that began in error. They were hatched by well-meaning people who would nevertheless manage to do a considerable public harm. And in this construal, the real vice for Peckham was the breach with laissez-faire. The offense was the interference with the rights of property and the regulation of business; but the shorthand expression that covered all of these sins was the abridgement of the "right to contract." That is the ground on which Peckham and the Court would strike down this law of New York State: that it interfered, unreasonably, with the freedom of workers to make contracts with their employers, to find the terms of employment that were suitable to their own interests, even if they did not accord precisely with the formulas of the legislation. To put it another way, the legislation might prescribe, as a rule of justice, a limit of ten working hours a day, or sixty hours a week. And yet, the legitimate, just interests of some workers could indeed be satisfied by working more than ten hours on certain days, and more than sixty hours in certain weeks. Or that at least was one of the lessons contained in the decision of the Court in the Lochner case. And for encompassing that modest point, among others, Peckham's decision would be stamped enduringly as "reactionary."

Of course, in the traditional liberal critique, the "right to contract" covered the freedom of vulnerable workers to make contracts with employers, who presumably had the upper hand. As it was often, and mockingly, put, the "liberty of contract" meant the liberty of workers to contract to work for more than sixty hours a week at less than a minimum wage. But judges a bit more seasoned in the world understood that there were times when employers, especially in smaller businesses, held little more bargaining power than their workers, for some of them were on the edge of losing their businesses and falling again into the ranks of the employed.[19]

Yet, that familiar cliché was hardly the least of the fictions that seemed to be absorbed as part of the critique of the so-called laissez-faire judges. If we looked back at those judges at the end of the

108

nineteenth century and the beginning of the twentieth—the so-called laissez-faire judges that Peckham and the *Lochner* case are taken to represent—we would find that, in every item in this list, the liberal critique did not get it right. In fact, we would find that the liberal critique was wrong at the center, wrong at the core; and once we are alerted to why it was wrong, we may suddenly become alert to a whole structure in Peckham's opinion in *Lochner* that has gone remarkably unnoticed.

I may sound here like Chesterton, and in that case I should produce a subtitle such as "Seven or Eight Damnable Lies about the Laissez-Faire Judges." Principal among the truths to be told is that these were not really laissez-faire judges, at least as our own age understands the term. Indeed, they could not be, given the premises that underlay their jurisprudence. After all, they were not yet positivists or "legal realists"; they continued to think that there was a moral ground that underlay the law, and that there had to be a moral ground, especially, for rights, including the rights of property. But then it only stood to reason that the judges who understood a moral ground for the rights of property were quite alert to the moral limits on those rights.

No one was a fiercer defender of property rights in that Court of the late nineteenth century than the redoubtable Stephen J. Field, and no one was clearer about the maxim that marked the limit to those rights of property: *sic utere tuo ut alienum non laedas* [roughly translated: use your own for the sake of causing no injury to others]. Under this doctrine, Field and his colleagues were willing to uphold virtually any legislation that bore even a plausible connection to the health, welfare, or safety of the local populace. The hidden truth about the judges of "substantive due process" is that they used that weapon very rarely, that their operating inclination was to presume in favor of the validity of laws, and defer to legislators elected by the people. And so Field could suffer not the slightest strain in upholding laws that, say, ordered the closing of businesses on Sunday. He could be quite clear, as he put it, that these "[l]aws setting aside Sunday as a day of rest are upheld, not from any right of the government to legislate for the promotion of religious observances, but from its right to protect all persons

from the physical and moral debasement which comes from un-
interrupted labor."[20]

That sentiment was expressed in one of the cases emanating
from San Francisco, dealing with the regulation of laundries, and
that series of cases provides as clear and dramatic a statement of
my point here as any cluster of cases. In 1884, the Board of Supervisors in San Francisco passed a series of ordinances regulating
the location and operating hours of laundries. Since there was a
concentration of Chinese immigrants in this business, there
was some suspicion that these local measures were really covert
schemes to restrict the competition engendered by the Chinese.
But in two cases, in 1885, Justice Field wrote for the Court in sustaining the regulations as legitimate uses of the police powers.
The business of laundering required continuous fires, and since
the business was often run around the clock, the fires were maintained through the night. It seemed plausible to Field and his
colleagues that, in San Francisco, "a city subject, . . . the greater
part of the year, to high winds, and composed principally within
the limits designated of wooden buildings, that regulations of a
strict character should be adopted to prevent the possibility of
fires. That occupations in which continuous fires are necessary
should cease at certain hours of the night would seem to be . . . a
reasonable regulation as a measure of precaution."[21] The judges
could not entirely discount the possibility that the legislation
might have been animated by a certain hostility toward the Chinese; but the measure itself was cast in general terms, and it created no classifications that would create disabilities mainly for the
Chinese. As Field pointed out, "No invidious discrimination is
made against any one by the measures adopted. All persons engaged in the same business within the prescribed limits are
treated alike and subject to similar restrictions."[22]

But the evidence for that "invidious" enforcement of the law
would soon come before the Court, and it would move the judges
to an entirely different judgment. Just a year later, in the case of
Yick Wo v. Hopkins, the Court considered another part of the regulations, which gave a different complexion to the laws. This part of
the ordinances created tiers of distinctions: laundries housed in

buildings made of brick and stone would be allowed to operate without restrictions. Laundries contained in wooden buildings would be subject to a different regimen. The owners would have to apply for a license to the Board of Supervisors, who could grant or withhold licenses based on their judgment of the applicant. But there was apparently no need for the supervisors to justify their decisions or give reasons that could be examined in a court. As the Supreme Court saw the case, the procedures were arranged then to invite the most "arbitrary" judgments, which did not have to be articulated or justified. As Justice Matthews wrote for the Court, the ordinances did "not prescribe a rule and conditions for the regulation of the use of property, for laundry purposes, to which all similarly situated may conform." But rather, the ordinance permitted the authorities to assign or withhold the freedom to work at a legitimate job, "merely by an arbitrary line."

The procedures bore all the earmarks of arbitrariness, and the results confirmed the suspicions: the only attribute that connected Yick Wo and the two-hundred other applicants rejected by the Board was that they were Chinese. Of the eighty applicants approved by the Board, none was Chinese.[23] The laws might have been fair in their construction, but as Justice Matthews wrote, the laws were administered with "a mind so unequal and oppressive as to amount to a practical denial by the State of the equal protection of the laws."[24]

Justice Field and his colleagues had made it clear, in these cases, that they were not lusting to draw power to themselves and make themselves into superintendents of the police powers in San Francisco. The same moral premises that fired them with a sense of injustice on behalf of Yick Wo also enjoined them to hold back their hands and respect the limits that were rightfully placed by local authorities on the uses of private property. The judges were prepared to credit even the most bumbling efforts at local management, as long as those efforts seemed to be directed earnestly to the legitimate ends of the police powers.

Regulations of business, then, raised no moral strains for the judges. But they also had the wit to recognize those gradations by which a law advertised as a regulation of business turned itself into something else. The judges were not vindicating rights of property in any narrow sense when they sought to protect the rights of aliens and Chinese to practice an ordinary calling, and they managed to notice the same vice at work in 1915, when the state of Arizona required that any establishment employing five or more workers had to reserve 80 percent of the jobs for native-born citizens of the United States. The measure was advertised, of course, as regulation of business in favor of a social policy—a determination to impose, as they say, "community values" against the prospect of an unregulated capitalism. But this kind of measure should not have been seen as a regulation of business any more than the Nazi legislation in the 1930s that sought to drive Jews from the professions and even from ordinary occupations. It was an expression, rather, of nativism, and in some cases, of racism. The case was called *Truax v. Raich*,[25] and what the Court saw in this case from Arizona was Mike Raich, an immigrant from Austria, prevented from working at an ordinary job in a restaurant. The Court would vindicate Raich's rights in this case, but this decision would be charged to the record of the conservative Court in its willingness to fend off the regulation of business.

I suggest that it is not merely an incidental connection that the same labor laws at issue in the Lochner case *also* contained a component that required positions in public employment to be reserved to American citizens. In the issue of the *New York Times* reporting on the decision of the Supreme Court in the Lochner case, there was also an account of a report submitted by the State Commissioner of Labor, noting with concern that over 60 percent of the employees in New York City were aliens, violating the labor laws of the state. The concern of the unions was deepened when the corporation counsel in the city had concluded that the law was a nullity, at least in regard to Italian immigrants—not on constitutional grounds, but because the law might have violated a treaty with the Italian government.[26]

This kind of legislation ran well beyond the breadth of tolerance that the judges were willing to accord to legislation that bore even a plausible connection to public health and safety. It would have been a caricature at war with understanding to characterize the reactions of the courts as a reflex simply to guard businesses against regulation. But at the same time, the judges saw nothing denigrating in the notion that they were defending rights of property, for those rights were indeed natural rights or human rights: the right to make a living at an ordinary calling, to enter a legitimate occupation without arbitrary restrictions, was a right that ran as deep as the right to speak or publish. And for ordinary men and women, who were not writers or intellectuals, it might be the right that bore on their lives with a more evident, palpable effect. In his dissenting opinion in the famous *Slaughterhouse* cases, Justice Field cited in this vein a decree issued by Louis XVI in France and written by his estimable finance minister, Turgot. In that decree, the king would dismantle the system of monopolies granted by the state and recede in this power of the state out of a respect for the natural rights of his subjects in the control of their own labor. The explanation in the edict took this form:

> [S]ome persons asserted that the right to work was a royal privilege which the king might sell, and that his subjects were bound to purchase from him. We hasten to correct this error and to repel the conclusion. God in giving to man wants and desires rendering labor necessary for their satisfaction, conferred the right to labor upon all men, and this property is the first, most sacred, and imprescriptible of all. . . . [Therefore, he regarded it] as the first duty of his justice, and the worthiest act of benevolence, to free his subjects from any restrictions upon this inalienable right of humanity.[27]

To recognize, in this way, the "natural right" of the worker to his own labor was to recognize that his labor did not belong to the state—or to his employer. It meant, as the first Justice Harlan once explained, that every person had a natural right "to sell his labor upon such terms as he deems proper," and a right "to quit the service of the employer for whatever reason."[28] He could be committed only on the basis of a contract, entered into freely. For the judges who came out of the antislavery movement, the notion of liberty of contract was another way of recognizing that a man had a primary claim to the ownership of his own labor, as he had a natural claim to the ownership of himself. For these judges, the

113

notion of "liberty of contract" was freighted with the same moral significance that attached to the notion of government "by the consent of the governed."

It is curious, in this respect, that when the Thirteenth Amendment was revived in the late 1960s, it was associated with the notion of "contract": as the argument ran, the refusal of private schools, or private companies, to accept black people as clients or customers marked a refusal to enter into contracts with blacks. Therefore it marked a refusal to treat black people with the dignity that attaches to a moral agent, a person competent to enter into contracts, a person who deserves to have his consent sought before he is committed.[29] It is curious that this "liberty of contract," in the hands of judges in the 1960s and 1970s, is regarded as the mark of a heightened, liberal sensibility. And yet the same concept, understood by judges like Sutherland, Harlan, Peckham in precisely the same terms, was taken as the mark of reactionaries. The matter might have been crystallized in this way: a right to contract could be claimed only by a "moral agent," as James Madison put it, a being who could deliberate about the grounds for offering, or withdrawing, his consent. But by the same token, moral agents had access to the understanding of right and wrong, and therefore they would also understand the ends they had no right to pursue, even through the device of a contract. With that understanding, the judges were explicit in pointing out the places in which a person's liberty of contract was very much open to the restraints of the law.

And so, Justice Sutherland could say, unequivocally, that "[t]here is, of course, no such thing as absolute freedom of contract. It is subject to a great variety of restraints. . . . The liberty of the individual to do as he pleases, even in innocent matters, is not absolute. It must frequently yield to the common good."[30] In *Lochner*, Peckham would take the matter to its moral root: he would defend the liberty of contract, but he would note at the same time that "[t]he State . . . has the power to prevent the individual from making certain kinds of contracts . . . [e.g.,] a contract to let one's property for immoral purposes, or to do any other unlawful act."[31] In the jural world of Rufus Peckham and his colleagues, the judges could never be called on to enforce a contract for prostitution or the "contract" to carry out a murder.

But once those moral premises were in place, it was quite clear that the law would be justified in restraining, at many points, the freedom of people to inflict harms through their uses of property, and the law would be amply warranted even in restraining a person from injuring himself through his own freedom to contract. Peckham would be charged with a certain flippancy in his willingness, in the Lochner case, to strike down the policies of a state. Yet, if we look closely at the structure of his argument, we would notice that he was careful to establish the framework by setting in place first, in all of its layers, the legitimate grounds on which the law may restrict or constrain the liberty of contract. In laying the groundwork in this way, he *assigned the burden of proof to any judge* who would overturn the policies of the legislature. It is worth recalling, then, even in a sketchy summary, the regulations that this supposed model of a laissez-faire judge was willing to uphold as legitimate:

- The limiting of working hours, in underground mines, to eight hours per day ("except in cases of emergency, where life or property is in imminent danger").

- The limiting of hours of work in smelting plants, where a prolonged exposure could pose risks to the health of workers [*Holden v. Hardy* (1897)].

- The requirement, by a state, that the owners of mines redeem coal for cash when workers are paid in kind [*Knoxville Iron v. Harbison*].

- The provision of vaccinations in a compulsory way, as part of a policy directed to "the public health and the public safety" [*Jacobson v. Massachusetts*].

- The requirement that barbershops and other establishments be closed on Sundays, even though a policy of that kind, too, would limit the hours that people were free to work [*Petit v. Minnesota*].[32]

Peckham found in most of these policies an earnest interest in protecting workers from fraud and hazards, and in promoting

115

public health. The question then was whether this law in New York was aimed plausibly at the public health. As I have suggested, Peckham approached this question with a discipline imparted to him from the traditions of the Court, a discipline in which he was prepared to credit any tenable connection to the public health along with an apt sympathy for the people who were the objects of protection. But that discipline also brought an aversion to subterfuge and a willingness to test, with a critical eye, the restrictions that were imposed upon personal freedom. That sense of freedom, in the understanding of Peckham, was never niggling, narrow, or confined to matters of property. In *Allgeyer v. Louisiana* in 1897, Peckham articulated one of the most expansive understandings of the range of personal freedom protected under the Fourteenth Amendment:

> The liberty mentioned in that amendment means not only the right of the citizen to be free from the mere physical restraint of his person, as by incarceration, but the term is deemed to embrace the *right of the citizen to be free in the enjoyment of all his faculties*; to be free to use them in all lawful ways; to pursue any livelihood or avocation, and for that purpose to enter into all contracts which may be proper, necessary and essential.[33]

H. L. Mencken once remarked on the curious illusion spun by Justice Holmes that induced the liberals to believe so readily that he was one of them. "The Liberals," he wrote, "who long for tickling with a great and tragic longing, were occasionally lifted to the heights of ecstasy by the learned judge's operations, and in fact soared so high that they were out of earshot of next day's thwack of the club."[34] And what the illusion camouflaged, in this instance, was that Peckham was far more of a libertarian, or a votary of "rights," than Holmes would ever be. I recall that when I read this case again in graduate school, I wondered how I could have been so dazzled by Holmes that I had missed the real dissent in the case, written by Justice Harlan and joined by two other colleagues. Holmes had been aphoristic, but Harlan had taken the trouble to lay out an argument, to cite the precedents, to frame the problem far more carefully. But then I must record my deeper surprise and embarrassment that when I returned to this case several years ago, I discovered that there was nothing in the main body of Harlan's argument that Peckham had not already encompassed—and arranged much more tellingly—in his opinion for the majority. When it came to setting in place the moral and constitutional justification for regulating commerce or placing restrictions on contracts, Peckham, as I have already shown, had done it all, and he had done it even more sharply than Harlan. The principal difference between Peckham's opinion and Harlan's was that Harlan had cited reports, or studies, on the hazards that might be facing bakers. He had cited, for example, a study by a Professor Hirt on "The Diseases of Workers," in which it had been remarked that "the labor of the bakers is among the hardest and most laborious imaginable." Why? Because that labor required a "great deal of physical exertion" in an "overheated workshop," and with the need, often, to perform the work at night, "thus depriving [the worker] of an opportunity to enjoy the necessary rest and sleep, a fact which is highly injurious to his health."[35] Harlan seemed to think it appropriate also to dip into the history of maladies for bakers, suggesting that bakers were somehow more susceptible to diseases that swept the community (perhaps because they might have been responsible in the past for spreading those diseases). In any event, he recalled that, in 1720, when the plague ravaged the city of Marseilles, "every baker in the city succumbed to the epidemic."[36]

But to rework an old phrase, what was novel in Harlan's opinion was no longer true, and, in fact, it was not even new. It was outdated. There had been much revision of late in the treatises on occupations, and there had also been some notable changes in the operations of bakeries since the plague had visited Marseilles. The kneading of dough was done mainly by machinery, especially in an establishment like the National Biscuit Company on 10th Avenue in New York, covering two city blocks. When the kneading was done by machinery, there was much less flour dust in the air, and even when the dust *was* there, the medical authorities were rather divided on the question of whether this state of affairs was really hazardous. One treatise, in the 1890s in England, published the mortality figures in different occupations, and when they were listed in descending order, moving from the most to the least hazardous, bakers held no prominent place on the list. They were down in the middle of the rankings, well beyond coal miners and brewers, laborers on docks, and even servants in inns.

There was, of course, a serious concern for health that bore on the sanitary conditions within the bakery as it affected not only bakers, but the public that consumed the products of the bakeries. Peckham never questioned the aptness of these laws, and indeed Lochner himself, and his lawyers, had never contested them. In fact, they conceded them readily, for they thought the regulations formed a dramatic contrast with the rules that were being brought forth now under the guise of the police power. And so the lawyers for Lochner pointed out the provisions that had been put in place, quite rightly, to specify the dimensions of the rooms, the air space and ventilation, the exclusion of domestic animals, the separation of the workplace from sleeping quarters and privies.[37] As Peckham noted, the legislature had already done, in this respect, "all that it could properly do":

> These several sections [of the law] provide for the inspection of the premises where the bakery is carried on, with regard to furnishing proper wash-rooms and water-closets, apart from the bakeroom, also with regard to providing proper drainage, plumbing and painting; the sections, in addition, provide for the height of the ceiling, the cementing or tiling of floors, where necessary in the opinion of the factory inspector, and for other things of that nature.[38]

But once these provisions were in place, the plaintiff and the judges were warranted in putting the question, in a demanding way, as to why the law should assume that it would be injurious, under any conditions, for a baker to work more than ten hours in any day. As Peckham pointed out, the law was written in such a way that it precluded even the employee who might be willing to work additional hours for especially generous, overtime pay.[39] These points of dubiety could be registered here, and they were given a deeper resonance by the terms of the statute that finally embarrassed the claims of this legislation as a health measure: according to an official report from the Factory Inspector's Bureau in New York, 3,828 bakeries were inspected in the state in 1897. Of that number, more than half employed only two, one, or no journeymen bakers.[40] That is, half of the establishments were so small that the owners themselves, or their families, did the baking. And by the terms of the laws, the owners and their families were not covered by these regulations, since they were classified as employers rather than employees. But as the lawyers for Lochner aptly argued, if this was a health measure that was to be imposed even on the worker who wished to work overtime, why was it not applied to the owners and their families? If it were really hazardous for people to work more than ten hours, why was there no concern to protect these small businessmen and their families? Then, too, why only the bakers who plied their trade in bakeries? There were people who did precisely the same work baking in hotels, restaurants, clubs, boardinghouses, and even in private households.[41] Yet the law did nothing to protect these people, who had to be, as we say, "similarly situated."

It appears that the concern of the law was not with the people who worked for long hours near ovens, but with the people who were more likely to be employees and members of the bakers' union. The first call for this restriction of hours had emanated from a meeting of bakers in 1887. It may be a telling sign of the forces behind this legislation that the law's principal effect seemed to be in reducing the number of small bakeries, which were of course marked by their want of need for union labor or their inability to afford it. As Bernard Siegan noted, the law seemed to advance the concentration of the baking business by enlarging the portion of sales taken by the larger, more corporate factories such as the National Biscuit Company.[42]

Whatever we may think of the motives that lay behind this legislation, I think we must concede that the judges had ample grounds for considering the argument on the basis of health to be immanently implausible. One might indeed have made a case on the issue of health, but evidently the legislators themselves were not honoring that case or taking it seriously. Of course, the judges might have relaxed the stringency of their inquiry or decided to be affably credulous. But the problem, as Peckham explained, was that the Court could not back itself into a rule of this kind: that it would lapse into a state of benign credulity if a legislature merely invoked the magic words and avowed that any measure was passed out of a concern for "the morals, the health or safety of the people." If the Court were prepared to sustain any piece of legislation so long as those phrases were uttered as invocations, then "the Fourteenth Amendment would have no efficiacy and the legislatures of the State would have unbounded power."[43] Or to put it another way, a review by the courts would become a ceremony evacuated of its substance, and what would be lost here is the very notion of a government restrained by a constitution.

Still, Peckham had not exhausted the possibilities for salvaging this legislation. Even if the rationale on the grounds of health was not compelling, the legislation could be regarded as a species of labor law, designed to protect workers who were vulnerable to the power of the employers. But the most telling markers were again absent: the workers here were not composed mainly of children or aliens, of people who were rendered vulnerable by their immaturity or ignorance or their want of legal standing as citizens. It has been common, of course, to presume that workers as a class were simply vulnerable to the overwhelming power of people called "employers." But judges who bore some experience in the world knew how problematic those suppositions could be. Half of the employers and their families were barely distinguishable from their employees, and many of them were working with such low overheads and low margins that they possessed very little leverage in regard to their workers. There were also periods of tight labor markets, in which workers could be choosy, or they could at least have a certain choice in avoiding situations they regarded as far less congenial. The differentials in compensation already indicated that it was necessary to pay people more to enter certain hazardous occupations than to work, say, in libraries or publishing houses.

Under those conditions, judges who were quite sympathetic to the purposes of the law might well wonder whether the law, in this case, was far too sweeping and categorical: whether it was injurious or profitable for a worker to work overtime in a bakery would depend on the age, the health, and the situation of the worker. No one could estimate these things more precisely than the workers themselves. What I am suggesting then is that even judges who were concerned about protecting workers could see something quite presumptuous—and quite harmful to the interests of working men and women—in legislation that swept in such an undiscriminating way and imposed the same restrictions in circumstances that admitted a host of plausible exceptions.

Against this prospect, Peckham was disposed to assume that bakers bore as much natural wit as anyone else. His own inclination was to presume that ordinary men and women had the competence to know their own interests and make their own judgments about the terms of employment that met their needs and merited their consent. With the presumption set in that direction, the judge would need to find compelling reasons to reach a different conclusion about bakers. But what was at stake here, in the understanding of Peckham and his colleagues, ran well beyond the situation of bakers. If the law could move, shall we say, less than rigorously in this case, it would be hard to distinguish bakers from many other classes of employees, and the reach of the law could end up astonishing even people with the most benign view of regulation. "No trade," said Peckham, "no occupation, no mode of earning one's living, could escape this all-pervading power":

> In our large cities [he continued] there are many buildings into which the sun penetrates for but a short time in each day, and these buildings are occupied by people carrying on the business of bankers, brokers, lawyers, real estate, and many other kinds of business, aided by many clerks, messengers, and other employes. . . . It might be said that it is unhealthy to work more than [a certain number] of hours in an apartment lighted by artificial light during the working hours of the day; that the occupation of the bank clerk, the lawyer's clerk, the real estate clerk, or the broker's clerk in such offices is therefore unhealthy.

. . . Not only the hours of employes, but the hours of employers, could be regulated, and doctors, lawyers, scientists, all professional men, as well as athletes and artisans, could be forbidden to fatigue their brains and bodies by prolonged hours of exercise.[44]

I know more than a few youngsters who have been put off from the profession of law by the prospect of working sixteen-hour days, and eighty- to ninety-hour weeks. We also know of many young people in the academy, working for their tenure, preparing for classes and working on manuscripts, who cannot practicably put a ten-hour limit on their working days. It is not merely that the law does not seek to rescue these young people from these regimens, but that we can hardly imagine a law that would try to regulate these matters by finding a formula that would apply even to all people within the same profession. Whether a young scholar needs to work to 1 A.M. may have something to do with his own powers of concentration, with the presence or absence of writing blocks. A law that sought to confine his limit to ten hours may not deliver him from his trials of learning or serve his interests. In the meantime, his willingness to put in the longer hours may conduce more readily to his well-being. If we are open here to some personal testimony, I can report that, as a teacher and writer, I can do, with far more dispatch, in my fifties what took me far longer to do as a young, new professor in my twenties. And yet, if I had been barred from putting in the additional hours, I would have been barred also from the kind of practice that I needed as a writer.

I know, of course, that we are inclined to make a distinction between the work chosen by academics and the work we may be inclined to regard as rather more prosaic, such as the work done in bakeries. But judges like Peckham seemed to recognize that even people in prosaic callings may find it just as useful to have the same freedom that we tend to reserve for the professional classes and to people—how shall I put this?—who are more like us.

The things we have simply folded here into our assumptions may supply a path through the puzzle, and if we followed it, we may be surprised to discover, at the end, that we have come to see the landscape in a strikingly different way. Let us suppose, in that vein, that there really was legislation that sought to protect professors and young lawyers in the way that the laws in New York had sought to protect bakers. Let us suppose that young professionals were barred by law from spending more than ten hours per day at their new professions. Does anyone doubt that some of these young professionals would be in court at once to challenge such a law? But more than that, could anyone really doubt today how the courts would rule on this issue? There could hardly be any question that the law would encounter the deepest dubiety of the judges, and that it would bear the heaviest burden of justification. We can virtually take it as a certainty that a law of that kind could not survive these days in the courts. But when we unpack the understandings that have evidently settled in, do we not get a clearer reading of the jural landscape? For now we presume that these kinds of cases may form the legitimate business of the courts, that the principles of the Constitution would be set strongly against such laws. Is that not a telling sign that Hugo Black has lost and Peckham has prevailed? Our law does not move in the cast defined by Black, in his opposition to substantive due process; our law moves today, more surely, in the cast of *Lochner*.

In our own day, I suspect we could hear claims about the maladies that are endemic to modern work in an office, even among young professionals. We may receive accounts of remarkable precision about "carpel tunnel syndrome" or the strain on the eyes suffered by people compelled to put in longer hours staring at computer screens and hammmering away at keyboards. Whether those injuries are any more or less serious than the injuries facing bakers, I could not say. My own inclination would be to say, with Peckham, that individuals will be the best judges of the things that cause them strain, and I would leave them the widest freedom for making their own adjustments. But having said that, or marked my own dubiety, I would not claim that the issue is unarguable: perhaps the hazards in baking are more severe than it seems to me after a detached view of the record. Or perhaps the people working in these establishments were more vulnerable, or far more in need of the sheltering of the law, than it appeared to Peckham and his colleagues at the time. I would preserve the possibility that, in these estimates, Peckham and his colleagues might have reckoned wrongly, or that they might have tipped their judgment, quite as plausibly, to the other side.[45] But my point is that even if we quarrel with their judgment in *Lochner* or balance the equities in a different way, it would not be because we would be acting on moral premises strikingly at odds with those of Peckham and his colleagues, or because we could bring to the project a wider sympathy for working people than they could encompass.

In fact, one of the ironies here is that, if we sought to mount a criticism of Peckham and *Lochner*, it could only be by establishing the ground of judgment that Peckham himself had been so fastidious in setting into place. The situation recalls that fetching passage that Rousseau struck off in the course of his defense of his First Discourse and offered in response to some criticisms that were composed by the king of Poland. Rousseau remarked that one of the most illustrious popes had once maintained that it was quite an honest and plausible thing to assert the word of God even against the rules of grammar. And yet, he said, of the people carried away in the torrents of this argument: "ils furent contraints de se conformer eux-mêmes à l'usage qu'ils condamnaient"—they were constrained to conform themselves to the usage they had condemned. And so, it was in a manner, as he said, "very knowing" (*très savante*) that most of them declaimed against the progress of science.[46]

The irony here is that, if we sought today to quarrel with Peckham, it could only be on the basis of the jural groundwork he had written so precisely to sustain. It could certainly not be on the grounds of the positivism that led Oliver Wendell Holmes and Hugo Black to reject the jurisprudence of *Lochner*. And after all, if we credit that litmus put forth earlier as the mark of modern liberal jurisprudence, the critique offered by Holmes and Black was based on a jurisprudence that surely would have yielded the "wrong" result in *Roe v. Wade*. In that reckoning, I suppose,

Holmes and Black would have to be charged with getting it wrong. The devotees of modern liberal jurisprudence may not find *Lochner* congenial, but it is not clear that they can assemble any moral argument against it.

As for Rufus Peckham, I wish I could tell you that my researches had turned up something in his private papers that might dislodge or confirm the characterization that Holmes had offered of him. But even if it were true that his major premise was "God damn it," we can piece together enough from his writings to say that, as a reigning aphorism, it still marked an outlook that made him notably different from several people I know in the academy who have made, as their own reigning aphorism, "God is dead." I was doing a piece for a magazine on the Holocaust museum, and as I turned into one hall, I encountered a vast bin filled with shoes. They were the shoes left by the victims, as the Nazis sought to extract anything in their possessions that might be used or sold. And for some reason, at that moment, what came flashing back was that line from Justice John McLean, in his dissenting opinion in the *Dred Scott* case: "A slave is not mere chattel. He bears the impress of his Maker, and is amenable to the laws of God and man; and he is destined to an endless existence."[47] The Nazis looked at their victims and thought that the real "durables" were the shoes. But of course, the people who begin with the premise that "God is dead" are no more able to make McLean's arguments or see the black victims in the way that McLean saw them. And though they may be people capable of the widest social sympathy, they may be hard put to explain why that forked creature, who walks on two legs and conjugates verbs, is anyone who can claim a special "sanctity" for his life, or be the bearer of what we call "rights."

Rufus Peckham may not have been a clubby fellow, but we can say of him at least this: he had the most firmly grounded sense that even working people, in the most ordinary and prosaic occupations, merited a presumption of their competence to govern their own lives; that they would not find in our patronizing tenderness the main security for their lives; and they surely would not find there the source of their rights.

NOTES

1. Robert Bork, *The Tempting of America* (New York: Free Press, 1990), 44.

2. As Matthews wrote, in a moving passage, "the law itself [might] be fair on its face," and yet "it [was] applied and administered by public authority with an evil eye and an unequal hand." *Yick Wo v. Hopkins* 118 U.S. 356, at 373–74 (1886).

3. Webster, argument for the plaintiff in *Dartmouth College v. Woodward*, 17 U.S. (4 Wheaton) 518, at 581–82 (1819).

4. Blackstone had regarded it as a solecism on the part of Mr. Locke to contend that "there remains still inherent in the people, a supreme power to alter the legislative, when they find the legislative act contrary to the trust reposed in them; for when such trust is abused, it is thereby forfeited." Quoted by Blackstone in *Commentaries on the Laws of England* (Oxford: Clarendon Press, 1765), book 1, p. 157. But what Blackstone regarded as a "chimera," James Wilson was willing to take now as part of the foundation of the American law. In his redoubtable lectures on jurisprudence, Wilson insisted that the American law began with the recognition of natural rights, and therefore it began with the understanding that the positive law may not exhaust the tests of morality. In short, a regime founded on natural rights began with the awareness that there could indeed be an immoral law, and an immoral law had to call into question the obligation to obey the law. And so Wilson could argue, in a remarkable turn, that "a revolution principle certainly is, and certainly should be taught as a principle for the constitution of the United States, and of every State in the Union." Wilson, First Lecture on the Law, in *The Works of James Wilson*, ed. Robert Green McCloskey (Cambridge, Mass.: Harvard University Press, 1967; originally published in 1804), vol. 1, 79.

5. *Tyson & Brothers v. Banton*, 273 U.S. 418, 445–46 (1927).

6. Holmes in *Tyson & Brothers v. Banton*, 273 U.S. 418, at 445–46; cited by Black in *Ferguson v. Skrupa*, 372 U.S. 726, at 729 (1963).

7. James Wilson recorded that older understanding in the compelling way in his "Lectures on Jurisprudence" in the 1790s: "In the contemplation of law, [wrote Wilson] life begins when the infant is first able to stir in the womb. By the law, life is protected not only from immediate destruction, but from every degree of actual violence, and, in some cases, from every degree of danger." See Wilson, "Of the Natural Rights of Individuals," in *The Works of James Wilson*, vol. 2, 585–610, at 597.

8. 262 U.S. 390.

9. 268 U.S. 510.

10. 372 U.S. 726.

11. Ibid., at 729.

12. 431 U.S. 494.

13. Ibid., at 542.

14. See, in this vein, the exchange among Senators Trumbull, Fessenden, and Johnson during the debate over the Civil Rights Act of 1866 in *Congressional Globe*, 39th Cong., 1st Sess., vol. 36, part 1, 505; and the exchange between Trumbull and Senator Davis, in ibid., at 600. This understanding was also incorporated in some early cases, testing the laws on miscegenation under the Fourteenth Amendment. See *In re Hobbes*, 12 Fed. Cas. 262 (C.C.N.D. Ga., 1871), *State v. Gibson*, 36 Ind. 389 (1871), *State v. Hairston and Williams*, 63 N.C. 451 (1869), *Doc. Lonas v. State*, 50 Tenn. 287 (1871).

15. See *People v. Lochner*, 73 App. Div. [New York] 120 (1902), People v. Lochner, 177 N.Y. 145 (1904). In this recounting of the facts, I have found a more detailed account in the briefs for the plaintiff (Lochner) submitted by Frank Harvey Field, in Philip B. Kurland and Gerhard Casper (eds.), *Landmark Briefs and Arguments of the Supreme Court* (Arlington, Va.: University Publications of America, 1975), vol. 14, 654–99, at 654–56.

16. Under this construal, as O'Brien said, the law "makes it a crime for the master to permit his servant to do what the servant has a perfect right to do.... [T]he master must see to it, at the peril of committing a crime, that his servants are driven out of the building the moment the clock registers the requisite ten hours." See *People v. Lochner*, 177 N.Y. 145, at 176–78 (1904).

17. *Lochner v. New York*, 198 U.S. 45, at 75 (1905).

18. The line was confirmed by Charles W. McCurdy in his entry on Rufus Peckham in *Encyclopedia of the American Constitution*, eds. Levy, Karst, and Mahoney (New York: Macmillan, 1986), p. 1371. I'd like to thank Prof. John Robinson of the law school at Notre Dame, who supplied this reference, and confirmed what seemed apparent to me: that this line, which I had remembered from thirty-six years earlier, was not something that a twenty-year-old was likely to make up. Still, the reference merely confirms the line without, however, furnishing the source—and the fuller quotation. The mystery remains in the mists of the legend.

19. One recalls here George Sutherland's observation in *Adkins v. Children's Hospital*: "The law is not confined to the great and powerful

employers but embraces those whose bargaining power may be as weak as that of the employee. It takes no account of periods of stress and business depression, of crippling losses, which may leave the employer himself without adequate means of livelihood." See 261 U.S. 525, at 556 (1923).

20. *Soon Hing v. Crowley*, 113 U.S. 703, at 710.

21. Ibid., at 708; see also *Barbier v. Connolly*, 113 U.S. 27 (1885).

22. *Soon Hing v. Crowly*, at 708.

23. *Yick Wo v. Hopkins, supra*, note 2, at 374.

24. Ibid., 373–74.

25. 239 U.S. 33 (1915).

26. See the *New York Times*, April 18, 1905, 6.

27. Quoted by Field in *The Slaughter-House Cases*, 83 U.S. (16 Wallace), at 110–11n.

28. *Adair v. United States*, 208 U.S. 161, at 174.

29. See, for example, *Runyon v. McCrary*, 49 L. Ed. 2d 415 (1876).

30. *Adkins v. Children's Hospital, supra*, note 14, at 561.

31. *Lochner, supra*, note 17, at 53.

32. See the citations in ibid., at 54–56.

33. 165 U.S. 578, at 589 (1897); my italics.

34. H. L. Mencken, "Mr. Justice Holmes," in *The Vintage Mencken* (New York: Vintage Books, 1955), 189–97, at 195.

35. *Lochner, supra*, note 17, at 70.

36. Ibid., at 71.

37. See the briefs for the plaintiff (Lochner), *supra*, note 17, at 672.

38. *Lochner*, at 61–62. In an edition of *The Lancet* in 1895, two English sanitary experts laid out the model regulations in detail: "[The underground rooms should be] at least eight feet high and a minimum of 500 cubic feet of air space for each workman, and a special allowance for each gas jet. Walls must be kept smooth and dry. Window space must equal one-eighth of the floor and ventilation, light, drainage and lavatory accommodations must be such as to satisfy advanced modern requirements, floors should have nine-inch concrete and drains should be a foot deep lain in concrete." *Briefs, supra*, note 11, at 710.

39. *Lochner, supra*, note 17, at 52.

40. *Briefs, supra*, note 15, at 668.

41. Ibid., at 661–62.

42. See Siegan, *Economic Liberties and the Constitution* (Chicago: University of Chicago Press, 1980), 116–19. Siegan reports that, in 1899, only 2 percent of the baking establishments were owned by corporations, and

in 1919 the comparable figure was 7 percent. But in this period, the corporate bakeries enlarged their share of production from 28.7 to 51.8 percent. In the bakeries owned by corporations, the average number of employees was around forty-four, as opposed to a work force of less than three people in the businesses run by their owners. As Siegan estimates, the larger, corporate bakeries found it much easier to absorb the cost of the regulations that were imposed under the labor laws. They might have calculated then that the laws would have the benign effect of squeezing out many of the small, marginal bakeries, operating with very low overhead. As Siegan observes, "The reaction to *Lochner* might have been far less harsh had the critics recognized that the law probably would have reduced considerably the wages of many low-paid workers, and caused others to lose their jobs." Ibid., at 118.

43. *Lochner, supra,* note 15, at 56.

44. Ibid., at 59–60.

45. In the meantime, though, there is something to ponder in the report, offered by Bernard Siegan, that there were, in New York City, in the late 1970s, about eight-thousand Chinese workers in garment factories, working far longer than the hours stipulated in the law and at less than the minimum wage. Their situation was known to the authorities and the unions, and yet there was a willingness to look the other way, mainly because these people and their families needed the jobs and the income. See Siegan, *supra, note* 41, at 119–20.

46. "[C]e fût d'une manière très savante que la plupart d'entre eux déclamarent contre le progrès des sciences." Rousseau, *Discourse sur les sciences et les arts* (Paris: Garnier-Flammarion, 1971), 87.

47. McLean in *Dred Scott v. Sandford,* 19 Howard 393, at 550 (1857).

CHAPTER SIX

The Substance of Process:
Lochner v. New York

DONALD DRAKEMAN

WHILE I WAS WAITING to receive a copy of Hadley Arkes's excellent chapter, I was ruminating on the five great cases in American constitutional law selected for this volume. Three of the five clearly dealt with momentous issues of public policy: *Dred Scott* brought the court face to face with slavery; *Brown v. Board of Education* addressed racial segregation in public education; and *Roe v. Wade* confronted the issue of abortion.[1] Whether we like the results in all of these cases or not, it is easy to see why they would make the all-star list.

Now let's look at the other two, *Marbury v. Madison* and *Lochner v. New York*.[2] How many of us can actually remember the facts in *Marbury v. Madison*? Have we given much thought to whether Mr. Marbury was well qualified to serve as a justice of the peace for the county of Washington? Similarly, do we have strong views on whether bakers in New York should have been permitted to work more than ten hours in a day, which was the substantive issue in *Lochner*? The answer in each case, I think, is no. Neither the facts nor the social issues arising in those cases have stimulated much debate in the last century or two. Then why are they "Great Cases," standing side by side with cases about slavery, racial segregation, and abortion?

The answer is that both *Marbury* and *Lochner* are landmark cases because they represented historic judicial power plays. They say relatively little about baker's hours or justices of the peace but a great deal about who makes the rules in American government. We might not have had *any* great cases without *Marbury v. Madi-*

son, where Chief Justice John Marshall delivered the oft-quoted phrase: "It is emphatically the province and duty of the judicial department to say what the law is,"[3] setting up the process that would, in our time, make the Supreme Court the principal, and typically ultimate, interpreter of the Constitution. As the Court announced in the 1958 case of *Cooper v. Aaron, Marbury v. Madison* "declared the basic principle that the federal judiciary is supreme in the exposition of the law of the Constitution, and that principle has ever since been respected by this Court and the Country as a permanent and indispensable feature of our Constitutional system."[4] Without *Marbury,* the judiciary might well have become what Hamilton described as "the least dangerous" branch of the government, and we would have far fewer "great cases."[5]

And without *Lochner* or, at least, *Lochner's* approach to constitutional decision making, we probably could not have much of what is considered contemporary American liberal jurisprudence, as Hadley Arkes has described so carefully in the previous chapter. For while *Marbury* laid the foundation for the Supreme Court to hold itself out as the final arbiter of the meaning of the Constitution, *Lochner* seemed to stand for the proposition that the Court's interpretation of that great document could be broad and creative, looking beyond the text to the natural rights or fundamental values of the people. In *Lochner,* Justice Rufus Peckham opened the door for simple phrases like "due process" to serve as the constitutional foundation of innumerable substantive rights that have been proclaimed by the Supreme Court in the twentieth century.

Many commentators have wrestled with the kinds of interpretative issues that were raised in *Marbury* and *Lochner,* but few have done so as succinctly as Humpty Dumpty does in *Through the Looking Glass.* During a lexical disagreement with Alice, Humpty Dumpty proclaimed, "When I use a word, it means just what I choose it to mean—neither more nor less."[6] Thus, he operates in much the same way that the Court did in *Lochner* when Justice Peckham found a way to make a clause about "process" the font of *substantive* rights rather than just procedural rules. Doing so has led to a series of scathing sound bites, from Justice Oliver Wendell

Holmes' jibe about Herbert Spencer's social statics to John Hart Ely's colorful reminder that "'substantive due process' is a contradiction in terms—sort of like 'green pastel redness.'"[7]

In criticizing Justice Peckham's invention of substantive due process, Holmes and Ely, then, stand with Alice when she asks Humpty Dumpty "whether you can make words mean so many different things."[8] But in *Lochner,* Peckham lines up with both Chief Justice Marshall in *Marbury* and Humpty Dumpty who says, "The question is, . . . which is to be master—that's all."[9] As Arkes has told us, due process was then—and seems to be now—*substantive* because that's what the Supreme Court says it is, even if Ely tells us that such a thing is a contradiction in terms. If *Marbury* stands for the Court's power to interpret the Constitution, *Lochner* shows us how far that power can reach once the Court chooses to exercise it broadly.

Now let us return to Arkes's redeeming words for Justice Peckham. Arkes tells us that *Lochner* is, in fact, not dead and gone. Rather, he says, "We live today, firmly, within the cast of *Lochner.* . . . The structure of jurisprudence marked by that case is the structure that our judges . . . choose again . . . whenever they are faced with the need to choose. *Lochner* is our law, it marks the jurisprudence of our own day, even for people who profess to disagree with its result, and who may even fancy that they are rejecting it at its root."

Arkes has made a strong case for these statements, and I thought he might have been asked by Robert George to complete the midterm assignment for the legendary Constitutional Interpretation course in the Politics Department at Princeton. It is not uncommon for students in that course to be asked to review *Lochner* in the light of a more modern case such as *Roe v. Wade.* The students are led to focus on the legitimacy of judicial action to overturn legislative judgments in the absence of an explicit textual mandate in the Constitution. They have been told by numerous constitutional scholars that *Lochner* represents an example of improper "legislation by the judiciary," whereas they have read the works of many commentators who say that *Roe v. Wade* is a landmark case recognizing women's rights of autonomy and privacy. Is it possible, they are asked, to reject the Supreme Court's embracing of substantive due process in *Lochner* while simultaneously accepting a quite similar approach to constitutional interpretation in *Roe v. Wade?*

Faced with this exam question, students who favor a "prochoice" position on the issue of abortion struggle to be supportive of Justice Harry Blackmun's constitutional analysis in *Roe v. Wade* despite the fact that they have read Ely's dismissal of *Lochner* and substantive due process as "green pastel redness." And Ely himself has noted that while the Court in *Roe v. Wade* purported to "disavow the philosophy of *Lochner*, it is impossible candidly to regard *Roe* as the product of anything else." It then becomes a challenge to figure out why the fundamental values infused into the Constitution in *Roe v. Wade* are so different from the "liberty of contract" that was precious to Justice Peckham in *Lochner v. New York*. In short, the students are asked, if you like *Roe*, do you have to like the much derided *Lochner* as well?

In his chapter, Arkes seems to be taking a different tack. He has made an extremely articulate and persuasive argument that what Justice Peckham did was quite reasonable. That being the case, I wonder if it follows naturally from Arkes's analysis of *Lochner* that he would find the approach to constitutional interpretation (if not necessarily the result) in *Roe v. Wade* equally justifiable. In other words, if he likes *Lochner*, does he accept *Roe?* It seems that he does not, at least based on his recent support of a public pronouncement lambasting *Roe v. Wade* as antidemocratic. Not long ago, Arkes joined a public "Statement of Pro-Life Principle and Concern" stating that the "sweeping" abortion license . . . defined unilaterally by the Supreme Court without recourse to the normal procedures of democratic debate and legislation . . . wounded American democracy."[10] Now that Arkes has rehabilitated Justice Peckham and the Court's substantive due process rationale in *Lochner*, how can he deprecate *Roe* as antidemocratic at the same time?

It would also be interesting to hear Arkes address the issue of whether the appeals to fundamental rights found in either *Lochner* or *Roe* have made the Supreme Court, in Humpty Dumpty's words, the "master" of all, usurping the role of the other branches and the people in constitutional government. This kind of anti-*Marbury*/anti-*Lochner* charge has been leveled at the Supreme Court's constitutional jurisprudence recently from a number of different parts of the political spectrum, and by Arkes himself, who wrote just recently: "Whether the issue has been abortion, or euthanasia, or 'gay rights,' the courts have taken steps that were noticeable as novel or portentous. But these moves seemed to have struck no chord, no moral or religious nerve, running through the broad public." And as a result, he concluded, "In one issue after another touching the moral ground of our common life, the power to legislate has been withdrawn from the people themselves . . . and transferred by the judges to their own hands."[11] It would be interesting to hear how Justice Peckham's substantive due process can be redeemed while the more modern Court's use of similar techniques is so thoroughly rejected by Arkes.

NOTES

1. Dred Scott v. Sandford, 19 How. 393 (1857); Brown v. Board of Education of Topeka, Kansas, 347 U.S. 483 (1954); Roe v. Wade, 410 U.S.113 (1973).

2. Marbury v. Madison, 1 Cr. 137 (1803); Lochner v. New York, 198 U.S. 45 (1905).

3. Cranch 137, 2 L.Ed. 60 (1803).

4. Cooper v. Aaron, 358 U.S. 1 (1958).

5. In *Federalist* No. 78, Hamilton said that the judiciary "will always be the least dangerous to the political rights of the Constitution; because it will be least in capacity to annoy or injure them." *The Federalist* No. 78. (B. Wright, ed., 1961), 490.

6. Lewis Carroll, "Through the Looking Glass," in Philip C. Blackburn and Lionel White, eds., *Logical Nonsense: The Works of Lewis Carroll* (New York: G. P. Putnam's Sons, 1934), 205.

7. John Hart Ely, *Democracy and Distrust: A Theory of Judicial Review* (Cambridge, Mass.: Harvard University Press, 1980), 18.

8. Carroll, "Through the Looking Glass," 205.

9. Ibid.

10. "The America We Seek: A Statement of Pro-Life Principle and Conccrn," *First Things* 63 (May 1996): 40–44.

11. Ibid., 67: 18–20.

CHAPTER SEVEN

Brown v. Board of Education
and "Originalism"

EARL MALTZ

ANY LIST of great constitutional cases must include *Brown v. Board of Education*,[1] in which the Supreme Court forbade states to maintain schools that were segregated by race. The story of *Brown* begins soon after the Civil War, in the early Reconstruction era. Disturbed by Southern treatment of free blacks and white unionists and unsure of congressional power to deal with the problem, the Republican-dominated Congress adopted Section 1 of the Fourteenth Amendment. Section 1 begins by explicitly overruling *Dred Scott v. Sandford*[2] on the question of African-American citizenship, declaring all persons born in the United States to be citizens both of the nation and of the state in which they reside. It then prohibits states from abridging the privileges and immunities of citizens of the United States; depriving any person of life, liberty, or property without due process of law; and denying any person equal protection of the laws. This provision, together with the remainder of the Fourteenth Amendment, was then ratified by the required number of states, largely because Republicans made such ratification a prerequisite for the readmission of the ex-Confederate states.

Initially, African Americans derived little benefit from the Fourteenth Amendment. Dealing primarily with issues of federal power to enforce the amendment, the Waite Court typically gave section 1 a relatively narrow reading.[3] The Fuller Court, which followed, was even less receptive to the claims of racial minorities. Its 1896 decision in *Plessy v. Ferguson* is one of the most infamous in American history. In *Plessy*, the Court turned back an equal-protection challenge to a statute requiring local railway companics to maintain separate but equal facilities for whites and African Americans using their services. Rejecting the claim that the statute imposed a "badge of inferiority" on African Americans, Justice Henry B. Brown argued that "if this be so, it is not by reason of anything found in the act, but solely because the colored race has chosen to put that construction upon it." By contrast, in his famous but widely misunderstood dissent, Justice John Marshall Harlan asserted that "in respect of civil rights, common to all citizens, the constitution of the United States does not . . . permit any public authority to know the race of those entitled to be protected in the enjoyment of such rights." Even Harlan, however, was not arguing that segregation generally violated the Constitution; both the language of his opinion and his record in other cases (including one involving segregated schools) belie any such interpretation of his position. Rather, contending that public transportation facilities were the functional equivalent of roads, Harlan's view was that the Louisiana statute interfered with the right of African Americans to travel—one of the "civil rights" which is "common to all citizens."[4]

In any event, *Plessy* enshrined the doctrine of separate but equal in American constitutional law. In 1927, the Court unanimously concluded that the same principle was applicable to public education in *Gong Lum v. Rice*.[5] However, beginning in 1938 with *Missouri ex rel. Gaines v. Canada*[6] and ending in 1950 with *McLaurin v. Oklahoma State Board of Regents*,[7] the Court chipped away at segregation in higher education by holding the states to a very strict standard of equality in the opportunities provided to African Americans. At this point, under the leadership of Thurgood Marshall, the NAACP Legal Defense Fund decided to mount a direct challenge to the constitutional principles that allowed the maintenance of segregated schools. After winding its way through the lower courts, the challenge first came to the Supreme Court as *Brown v. Board of Education* on December 9, 1952.[8]

At that time the Court was under the leadership of Chief Justice Fred M. Vinson of Missouri. The first round of briefs and arguments left the Court deeply divided; while Justices Hugo L. Black, William O. Douglas, Felix Frankfurter, Harold H. Burton, and

Sherman Minton seemed ready to overturn *Plessy* and outlaw seg-regation in public schools, Frankfurter believed that Vinson, Stanley F. Reed, Robert H. Jackson, and Thomas C. Clark were inclined to dissent (although Jackson was apparently prepared to strike down segregation in the District of Columbia and to con-demn the practice as a policy matter).

All of the justices knew that a 5–4 or 6–3 decision that over-turned *Plessy* would be a recipe for major civil unrest. *Any* decision that attacked segregated schools was sure to meet with resistance from white southerners, and the position of the pro-segregation forces would be that much stronger if they could claim the sup-port of a number of the justices themselves. Thus, the Court de-cided to hold the case for new briefs and arguments, requesting the parties to specifically address the original understanding of the Fourteenth Amendment, as well as the remedial issues that would follow from a holding that the maintenance of segregated schools was unconstitutional.

The delay created an entirely new dynamic on the Court. Prior to reargument, Chief Justice Vinson died and was replaced by Governor Earl Warren of California. As a candidate for the Re-publican presidential nomination in 1952, Warren had been a wholehearted supporter of legislation to protect the civil rights of African Americans; not surprisingly, on the Court he proved to be a passionate opponent of segregated schools. Freed from Vinson's personal and professional influence, Tom Clark now informed his colleagues that he would vote to end segregation in schools. Robert Jackson also made clear his support for that view, although neither he nor Clark could find any warrant for their position in the original understanding. Now isolated, and understanding the practical consequences of filing a dissenting opinion, Stanley Reed chose instead to suppress his views. Thus, at 12:52 P.M. on May 17, 1954, Chief Justice Warren was able to announce that the Court had unanimously concluded that the maintenance of ra-cially segregated schools was unconstitutional.

Warren's opinion for the Court is a rather pallid affair, reflect-ing the need to maintain unanimity and avoid the filing of even concurring opinions. Warren begins by finessing the question of the original understanding, describing the evidence as "inconclusive." He then argues that, in any event, public education had far greater importance in 1954 than in the 1860s. Against this background, the opinion then cites psychological evidence to the effect that the maintenance of segregated public schools has a detrimental effect on African American children, and concludes that "in the field of public education, the doctrine of 'separate but equal' has no place [because] separate educational facilities are inherently unequal."[9]

Even after this clear holding, the question of the proper remedy for the constitutional infirmity remained unclear. In 1955, the Court placed the problem in the hands of local federal district courts with the admonition that the transformation from dual school systems to unitary systems should take place "with all deliberate speed." However, the process of transformation proved to be much more deliberate than speedy. Efforts to desegregate Southern schools met with stubborn resistance from state and local officials and (initially at least) only lukewarm support from other branches of the federal government. This resistance in turn generated a more combative attitude from the Supreme Court itself. In 1954, the most far-reaching possibility that the Court even considered was a decree requiring that "within the limits set by normal geographical districting, Negro children should forthwith be admitted to schools of their choice." By 1968, the Court had rejected the theory that freedom of choice was a sufficient remedy for past de jure segregation; in 1971, the principle of "normal geographical districting" also disappeared from the Court's jurisprudence, as district courts were authorized to use widespread transportation of students in an effort to achieve racial balance. Soon thereafter, the same principles began to be applied by the courts in school districts in northern cities, even where the school systems had never been formally segregated by law.[10]

Despite these innovations, the practical impact of *Brown* and its progeny on educational opportunities for African Americans has been less profound than some might have hoped. More than forty years after the decision, many African Americans continue to be educated in schools that are segregated in fact if not by law, many of which are chronically underfunded and beset by problems of violence and poverty. Not surprisingly, the level of achievement in these schools is often low. Faced with this reality, some critics have argued that the theory of *Brown* was fundamentally misguided, and that rather than emphasizing desegregation, the Court should have focused on the more general problem of equalizing and improving educational opportunities for African Americans.[11]

The true importance of *Brown*, however, must be understood in a broader context. *Brown* was the first case in which the Court clearly threw its weight against the Jim Crow system of segregation. Even if one discounts the practical impact of the Court's own efforts, *Brown* and its progeny were thus significant factors (indeed, perhaps indispensable factors) in creating the moral and political climate that produced the passage of the Civil Rights Act of 1964 and the Voting Rights Act of 1965—two statutes which have produced undeniable real-world changes.

Examining a wide variety of quantitative measures, Gerald M. Rosenberg has argued that the influence of the Court's decision on the political dynamic was minimal at best. Even Rosenberg's data, however, suggests that the confrontation in Little Rock—a direct result of *Brown*—had a significant impact on public awareness of the problems created by racial segregation. Moreover, Rosenberg makes no effort to compare the situation that actually existed in the wake of *Brown* with that which might have existed if the Court had rejected the constitutional challenge to de jure segregation.[12]

Consider the impact that a contrary decision in *Brown* might have had on the debate over the Civil Rights Act of 1964. In the Senate, the statute was passed only after a brutal political struggle, featuring a filibuster by southern senators that was broken on a close vote, and only after supporters of the bill had modified it to meet the objections of wavering senators. If the Court had rejected the challenge in *Brown*, the opponents of the bill could have claimed a constitutional imprimatur for the maintenance of the Jim Crow system—a claim that could only have strengthened their position and made the passage of a Civil Rights bill more difficult, if not impossible.[13]

In any event, the impact of the desegregation cases was not limited to simple changes in the political and social status of African Americans; *Brown* also marked the beginning of a new direction in the Supreme Court's constitutional analysis. Post-*Brown* jurisprudence has been marked by the development of a wide-ranging judicial activism that has gone well beyond the original understanding of the Constitution. Even in *Brown* itself, a number of the justices believed that their conclusions did not reflect the original understanding of the Fourteenth Amendment; however, the Court at least made some (admittedly disingenuous) effort to make the decision *appear* to be consistent with originalist theory. By 1966, however, a majority of the Court had abandoned all pretense of fidelity to the original understanding, relying on *Brown* for the proposition that "the Equal Protection Clause is not shackled to the political theory of a particular era. In determining what lines are unconstitutionally discriminatory, we have never been confined to historic notions of equality, any more than we have restricted due process to a fixed catalogue of what was at a given time deemed to be the limits of fundamental rights."[14]

Post *Brown* activism initially had a clear political orientation. In every case in which the Warren Court invoked the Constitution to strike down the action of another branch of government, it advanced the political agenda of the liberal wing of the Democratic party. Even during the chief justiceship of Warren Burger, the Court often determined that the Constitution embodied the political views of liberal Democrats and rarely held that the Constitution mandated results favored by conservative Republicans. Most often, the Burger Court decisions that were characterized as "conservative" concluded only that the Constitution left the government unconstrained by either liberal or conservative values.

Against this background, the debate over originalist methodology divided the country along political lines. Many conservatives attacked not only the substantive conclusions of post-*Brown* jurisprudence, but also the legitimacy of judicial activism that was not

141

founded on the original understanding. Liberals, on the other hand—ignoring the lessons of the pre-1937 *Lochner* era—increasingly saw an unconstrained Court as a reliable political ally; thus, originalism became anathema in liberal ideology.

The political debate over originalism reached its apex during the bitter struggle over the nomination of Robert Bork to the Supreme Court in 1986. The nomination was defeated because Bork's opponents were successful in characterizing him as a dangerous right wing extremist. Bork did not, however, advocate a return to *Lochner*-era jurisprudence; indeed, he explicitly and openly condemned that approach. Instead, Bork's mortal sin was arguing that the Court should be no more activist than mandated by the original understanding.

Brown has played a central role in the political and intellectual debate over originalism. Although extremely controversial when decided, the desegregation decision has become a constitutional icon; any person who advocates a theory that is inconsistent with the result in the case risks being branded either a fool or a racist. Thus, even Bork felt compelled to construct an originalist justification for *Brown*; other prominent originalists have made similar efforts.[15] The problem is that any attempt to defend *Brown* in originalist terms inevitably falls prey to an overwhelming mass of contrary historical evidence.[16]

Any accurate originalist analysis of *Brown* must begin with the understanding that, contrary to the views of many commentators, the language of Section 1 of the Fourteenth Amendment was not understood to be an open-ended appeal to general principles of justice and equality; rather, in the 1860s, privileges and immunities, due process of law, and equal protection of the laws were legal terms of art, unclear at the, margins, perhaps, but in general well defined by a substantial body of case law. Moreover, the framers themselves were well aware of this fact; the debates over Section 1 and its precursors are replete with discussions of both legal authority and the specific consequences of the use of particular language. For example, when queried about the meaning of the due process clause, Representative John A. Bingham, the author of Section 1, responded "the courts have settled that long ago, and the gentlemen can go and read their decisions."[17]

Against this background, the Republicans who drafted the Fourteenth Amendment deliberately rejected race-based language and chose instead language that more generally protected a limited set of rights. This choice was entirely consistent with the basic political ideology of the Republican party. Admittedly, Section 1 was aimed primarily at the treatment of the freed slaves in the South (although Republicans were also concerned with the position of white unionists). However, most Republicans did not believe that racial discrimination was wrong per se. Rather, they believed that African Americans were entitled to basic rights: first, because all persons were entitled to a certain set of natural rights; and second, because African Americans are citizens of the United States and as such are entitled to certain additional rights. Thus, as one prominent Republican put it in the late 1850s, granting African Americans fundamental rights was a question of manhood, not color.[18]

What were the rights to which citizens were equally entitled? Among the most basic was the right to protection of the laws. While fundamental, however, this right was understood to have a particularly narrow compass. It was not a guarantee of equal laws; instead, it was thought to essentially ensure only procedural protection of rights that were otherwise guaranteed by natural or positive law. This concept was so elementary that it was supported even by some who were generally opposed to guaranteeing civil rights to the freed slaves. Given this understanding, it should not be surprising that the guarantee of equal protection of the laws was not considered the most significant language during the debate over the Fourteenth Amendment. Instead, the privileges and immunities clause was generally believed to be the most wide-ranging and important provision in Section 1.

The difficulty with the privileges and immunities clause is that it does not protect privileges and immunities of *state* citizenship, but only those associated with *national* citizenship. This distinction is clearly reflected in the language of the Fourteenth

Amendment itself. While the amendment declares that "all persons born or naturalized in the United States . . . are citizens of the United States *and of the State wherein they reside*," the privileges and immunities clause protects only "privileges and immunities of citizens of the United States." Moreover, Republicans clearly recognized the import of this distinction. For example, Republican Representative William Lawrence of Ohio declared that "all privileges and immunities are of two kinds, to wit, those which [are] inherent in every citizen of the United States, and such others as may be conferred by local law and pertain only to the citizens of the state"; and Republican Representative Samuel Shellabarger of Ohio distinguished between "those local, and not fundamental, privileges . . . which a State may give to its own permanent inhabitants and deny to sojourners [and] 'fundamental' [rights which] cannot be taken away from any citizen of the United States by the laws of any State." In each case, Republicans identified the rights to be protected with those appurtenant to national citizenship.[19]

The right to attend public school was not viewed as such a right. Even when considered in the abstract, the right to a free public education fits comfortably into the mold of a right "conferred by local law and pertain[ing] only to the citizen of the State." Unlike (for example) the right to contract and to be free from bodily restraint, it cannot be viewed as a natural right that preexisted the establishment of governments. Unlike the right to hold real property, it is not the by-product of allegiance to a federal government with sovereign authority over that property. Instead, public education is a creation of each state government, supported by the local taxation for the benefit of its own citizenry. As such, access to public education is the quintessential example of a right dependent on state rather than national citizenship and is thus outside the protection of the privileges and immunities clause.

Any originalist defense of *Brown* must also contend with the historical context in which the Fourteenth Amendment was adopted. School segregation was common in the northern states during the period in which the Fourteenth Amendment was drafted and ratified. Segregation was particularly prevalent in the states of the lower North—the pivotal battleground states in

144

the national elections. Thus, any direct, broad-based effort to attack segregated schools would have carried with it substantial political risks.

The moderate Republicans who controlled the drafting of the Fourteenth Amendment were disinclined to take such risks. Although Section 1 is couched in terms of legal art, the amendment as a whole was in large measure a campaign document, designed to outline the Republican program of Reconstruction for the upcoming elections of 1866. As such, all of its provisions—including Section 1—were carefully drafted to appeal to swing voters in the post-Civil War electorate. As part of their strategy, mainstream Republicans repeatedly assured these voters that Section 1 would have only a minimal impact on northern state laws—a claim they could not have made if Section 1 had been generally understood to outlaw segregated schools.

The congressional treatment of the District of Columbia school system underscores the unwillingness of Republicans in the Thirty-ninth Congress to attack school segregation. Issues of federalism did not constrain congressional action dealing with the District of Columbia; thus, on issues such as streetcar segregation, voting rights, and jury service, mainstream Republicans in Congress acted to protect the rights of free blacks in the District well in advance of the passage of nationally applicable measures. By contrast, contemporaneously with the Fourteenth Amendment, the same Republicans continued to support the segregated school system in the District of Columbia. To contend that Republicans would at the same time knowingly act against school segregation by a nationally applicable constitutional amendment is to attribute to them an almost Orwellian mentality.

In short, *Brown* cannot be defended by reference to the original understanding. Thus, in order to remain an originalist, one must accept a constitutional order in which the federal courts would have been powerless to act against many aspects of the American system of apartheid. How can one defend such an approach to constitutional adjudication?

Originalists most commonly respond with a formal, essentialist argument. They contend that the Constitution is the only appropriate source of judicial power to invalidate state laws, and that the Constitution is itself only an embodiment of the will of the framers. Thus, when judges go beyond the original understanding, they impermissibly exceed the scope of their legitimate authority—even if the result in the case might be seen as desirable in the abstract.

This argument conforms with widely shared intuitions about the nature of law and the role of the judiciary in our system of government. Nonetheless, it does not conclusively refute non-originalist defenses of *Brown*. Nonoriginalists can respond simply that they have a different conception of the proper role of the judiciary, and that society will in fact function better if judges are empowered to intervene against government policies that they view as undeniably immoral, such as the maintenance of segregated schools.

If only the result in *Brown* were at stake, this functional argument would have great force. Obviously, today few people would argue that the states should be permitted to maintain schools that are segregated by law. However, *Brown* cannot be considered in isolation; if judges are freed from the constraints of originalism, history demonstrates that they will invoke the Constitution against a wide variety of actions that they find distasteful for one reason or another. Some of these decisions—like *Brown*—clearly changed America for the better; other nonoriginalist decisions, by contrast, express policies that remain controversial or are universally viewed as disastrous. The question is whether *on balance*, non-originalist activism has been or is likely to be a benefit to society. Put another way, the issue is whether justices of the Supreme Court are more competent to make basic political or moral judgments than members of other branches of state and federal governments.

Certainly there is nothing in the basic qualifications for appointment to the Supreme Court which suggests that the justices will be particularly adept in evaluating competing moral or political claims. Justices typically have no special training in disciplines such as philosophy, theology, anthropology, sociology, or political science, which might arguably provide the necessary expertise for such evaluations. Instead, the usual qualifications for nomination and confirmation are that the nominee be well connected politically; that he or she share the basic political philosophy of the president; and (if the nomination is to be considered a "good" one), that the person have demonstrated mastery in the art of manipulating technical rules of law. None of these qualifications suggests great insight into questions of morality or public policy.

Moreover, the historical record hardly supports the contention that the Court is institutionally well situated to make basic political and moral decisions. Even if only race-related cases are considered, nonoriginalist judicial activism has been at best a two-edged sword. This point emerges clearly if one juxtaposes *Brown* with *Dred Scott v. Sandford*[20] and *Shaw v. Reno.*

If *Brown* reflects the promise of judicial activism, *Dred Scott v. Sandford* just as surely reflects its dangers.[21] In *Dred Scott*, the Court concluded that Congress had no power to prohibit slavery in the federally governed territories, and that descendants of slaves could never become citizens of the United States. Certain aspects of the case bear an almost uncanny resemblance to *Brown*. In both cases, the Court was faced with a largely sectional dispute between white elites over the proper treatment of African Americans—a dispute that divided Democrats and ultimately split the party; in both cases, the Court determined that the views of one section of the country were written into the Constitution; in neither case was the decision consistent with originalist theory; and in both cases the opinion for the Court distorted history to make it seem that the decision was consistent with the original understanding (or at least, not completely inconsistent with that understanding). Of course, from our perspective the two cases differ in one very important respect: whereas Chief Justice Earl Warren got it right in *Brown*, Chief Justice Roger Brooke Taney got it precisely backwards in *Dred Scott*.

Ironically, in both cases, seven of the nine justices were members of the Democratic party. However, the orientation of the party itself changed dramatically between 1858 and 1954. The juxtaposition of *Dred Scott* and *Brown* clearly reflects this change in orientation.

In the late 1850s the question of the extension of slavery to the territories was the central issue in American politics. The Republican party was committed to the position that slavery should be banned from the territories; thus it should not be surprising that Republican John McLean dissented in *Dred Scott*, as did Benjamin Robbins Curtis, a Massachusetts Whig who had been left without a party by the political upheaval of the mid-1850s. By contrast, the Democratic party was divided between advocates of the Southern position—that slavery must be allowed in the territories—and those who favored the theory of popular sovereignty, which would have left the decision to the people of each territory.

Adherents to the Southern position dominated the *Dred Scott* Court. Five of the seven Democratic justices—Chief Justice Taney and Justices Peter Daniel, James M. Wayne, John A. Campbell, and John Catron—were citizens of slave states. The two northern Democrats—Samuel Nelson of New York and Robert Grier of Pennsylvania—were classic "doughfaces" whose sympathies were, in the words of Don E. Fehrenbacher, at least grimly anti-antislavery, if not actively pro-slavery.[22] Thus, it should not be surprising that all of the Democrats concurred in rejecting Dred Scott's argument for freedom.

White Americans were also deeply divided over the appropriate treatment of African Americans at the time *Brown* was decided. The Republican party still had little strength in the South, and many white Republicans agreed with Earl Warren's opposition to state-imposed segregation. As in the *Dred Scott* era, the Democratic party was split along largely sectional lines. Southern white supremacists remained an important Democratic constituency; indeed, until 1964, they were the most consistently loyal supporters of Democratic candidates at both the local and national level. However, beginning in the mid-1930s, national party policymaking was dominated by northern liberals who were opposed to state-imposed segregation. Four of the seven Democratic justices—William O. Douglas, Felix Frankfurter, Robert H. Jackson, and Sherman Minton—were drawn from this wing of the party. While the remaining three Democrats—Hugo L. Black, Thomas C. Clark, and even Stanley F. Reed—had southern roots, they might be described as "reverse doughfaces," rejecting the segregationist views espoused by the southern Democratic establishment. Thus, the unanimity of the Court in *Brown* reflected the fact that an important element in the American power structure was unrepresented on the Court.

This point emerges even more clearly when *Brown* is juxtaposed with *Shaw*. There, in 1993, the Court held by a 5–4 vote that racial considerations could not be the dominant factor in drawing legislative districts, even when the purpose was to ensure adequate representation for previously underrepresented minority groups. However one feels about the specific practice that was invalidated in *Shaw*, the decision highlights the problems created by abandoning the constraints of the original understanding.

First, the merits of the political philosophy reflected in *Shaw* remain highly controversial. The case thus reminds us that the proper resolution of the issues posed by cases such as *Brown* will generally be no less controversial at the time the decisions are rendered; a consensus on the "correct" answer in *Brown* emerged only in hindsight. However, judges cannot have the benefit of such hindsight when called upon to render a definitive judgment.

Moreover, the close division of the Court in *Shaw* emphasizes the political vagaries that can effect the Court's view on questions such as those presented in that case and *Brown*. The fifth vote in *Shaw* was provided by Clarence Thomas, a recent replacement for Thurgood Marshall, who certainly would have voted with the *Shaw* dissenters. Thus, the Court's decision to intervene depended on a number of almost random occurrences—George Bush's victory over Michael Dukakis in 1988, which presaged conservative appointments to the Court; the fact that Marshall's health failed in 1991, rather than late 1992, which would have allowed Bill Clinton to appoint his successor; and (quite possibly) the decision of a handful of Democratic senators to support Thomas's nomination, even in the face of the Anita Hill allegations.

More broadly, the Court's decision to intervene in *Shaw* reflected a sea change in American politics brought about largely by the civil rights revolution in which *Brown* acted as an important catalyst. While white southerners had shown evidence of dissatisfaction with the national Democratic party as early as 1948, it was the firm commitment to civil rights of President Lyndon Baines Johnson—ironically, a southerner himself—that ultimately drove a majority of them away from their traditional allegiance and into the Republican party. Here they found allies from other sections, alienated from the Democratic party by the efforts of the Supreme Court to impose racial balance on northern cities that had never been formally segregated by law and—perhaps most importantly—the general movement of the Democratic party away from the doctrine of racial neutrality toward the principle of race-conscious affirmative action. By 1980, this group, together with other social conservatives, was firmly in control of the national Republican party; moreover, beginning in that year they were instrumental in electing Ronald Reagan as president for two terms, and George Bush as president for one term. It is thus no accident that all five members of the *Shaw* majority—Chief Justice William H. Rehnquist and Justices Sandra Day O'Connor, Antonin Scalia, Anthony Kennedy, and Clarence Thomas—were appointed by either Reagan or Bush; and that three of the four dissenters—Byron R. White, Harry A. Blackmun, and John Paul Stevens—were selected by other presidents.

When viewed against the background of decisions such as *Dred Scott* and *Shaw*, *Brown* no longer appears as a shining example of the institutional competence of the Court to deal with questions of profound moral and political significance. Instead, the decision epitomizes a principle of common sense: judges who are unconstrained by the original understanding will simply constitutionalize the views of the particular segment of the ruling elite from which they are drawn. The case simply reflects a happy confluence of political circumstance that brought together a group of lawyers with a profound distaste for state-imposed racial segregation—just as *Dred Scott* and *Shaw* reflected the political beliefs held by the majority of the justices in those cases.

Let me hasten to add that I am not so naive as to believe that the decisions of judges who are committed to originalism will never be influenced by their political opinions. Where the passions of judges are deeply engaged, they will be prone to see what they want to see in the historical record, as *Dred Scott* demonstrates. Alternatively, they might engage in what David Strauss has described as a variety of civil disobedience, consciously choosing to ignore sound legal principles in order to avoid an extremely distasteful conclusion;[23] this seems to have been the course adopted by both Robert Jackson and Tom Clark in *Brown*.

However, in this respect, the significance of cases such as *Dred Scott* and *Brown* should not be overstated. The decisions do not demonstrate that, in the real world, originalism cannot be a meaningful constraint on the Supreme Court's treatment of constitutional issues. Instead, they reflect the fact that justices are human, and that under extreme ideological pressure they will occasionally rebel against even the most clearly defined rules of legal analysis. Conversely, in the vast majority of cases, a justice who is truly committed to originalism will be strongly constrained in his decision-making process—particularly if his personal commitment to originalism is supported by the legal culture generally.

However, since 1954, the prevailing legal culture has turned strongly against originalism. Seeking to legitimate *Brown* and other nonoriginalist decisions, leftist constitutional scholars—the dominant force in the academy—have deployed a wide variety of arguments in a concerted effort to conclusively discredit originalism as a theory of adjudication. Enthralled with the current makeup of the Court, influential conservatives have begun to espouse analogous positions. A full evaluation of the theoretical arguments against originalism is well beyond the scope of this lecture;[24] nonetheless, *Brown* itself provides an accurate glimpse of the future of constitutional interpretation in a nonoriginalist world. Considered in isolation, the result in the case was socially desirable; however, the decision was also the precursor of an era in which what passes for constitutional law is nothing more than a reflection of the values held by a majority of the nine lawyers who happen to be on the Court at a particular time. While some may find this regime congenial, I view it deeply disturbing.

NOTES

1. 347 U.S. 483 (1954).

2. 60 U.S. (19 How.) 393 (1857).

3. The Fourteenth Amendment jurisprudence of the Waite Court is described in Earl M. Maltz, "The Waite Court and Federal Power to Enforce the Reconstruction Amendments," Jennifer M. Lowe (ed.), *The Supreme Court and the Civil War* (Washington, D.C.: Supreme Court Historical Society, 1996), 75–88.

4. 196 U.S. 537 (1896) at 551, 554 (Harlan, J., dissenting). Examples of cases in which Harlan voted to countenance race-based classifications include Pace v. Alabama, 103 U.S. 583 (1883) and Cumming v. County Bd. of Election, 175 U.S. 528 (1899).

5. 275 U.S. 78 (1927).

6. 305 U.S. 580 (1938).

7. 339 U.S. 637 (1950).

8. The account which follows is taken from Richard Kluger, *Simple Justice* (New York, 1976).

9. Brown, 347 U.S. at 489, 495.

10. Brown v. Board of Education, 349 U.S. 294, 301, 298 n.2 (1955); Green v. County School Board, 391 U.S. 430 (1968); Swann v. Charlotte-Mechlenburg Board of Education, 402 U.S. 1 (1972); Keyes v. School Dist. No. 1, 413 U.S. 189 (1973).

11. Jennifer S. Hochschild, *The New American Dilemma: Liberal Democracy and School Desegregation* (New Haven, 1984), provides a detailed assessment of the benefits of integration for minority students.

12. Gerald Rosenberg, *The Hollow Hope: Can Courts Bring About Social Change?* (Chicago, 1991), at 114.

13. The legislative history of a key provision of the Civil Rights Act is described in detail in Frances J. Vaas, "Title VII: Legislative History," *Boston College Industrial and Commercial Law Review* 7 (1966): 431–458.

14. Harper v. Virginia State Bd. of Elections, 383 U.S. 663, 669 (1966).

15. Robert Bork, "Neutral Principles and Some First Amendment Problems," *Indiana Law Journal* 47 (1971): 1–35, at 11–15; Michael W. McConnell, "Originalism and the Desegregation Decisions," *Virginia Law Review* 81 (1995): 947–1140.

16. The discussion which follows is taken from Earl M. Maltz, "A Dissenting Opinion in *Brown*," *Southern Illinois University Law Review* 20 (1995): 93–98, and Earl M. Maltz, "Originalism and the Desegregation

Decisions—A Response to Professor McConnell," *Constitutional Commentary* 13 (1996): 223–32.

17. *Congressional Globe*, 39th Cong., 1st Sess. 1089 (1866).

18. Eric Foner, *Free Soil, Free Labor, Free Men* (New York, 1970), at 288–90.

19. *Congressional Globe*, 39th Cong., 1st Sess. (1866) at 1836, app. 293.

20. 60 U.S. (19 How.) 393 (1857).

21. The standard account of *Dred Scott* is Don E. Fehrenbacher, *The Dred Scott Case: Its Significance in American Law and Politics* (New York, 1978).

22. Ibid., 234.

23. David A. Strauss, "'Tragedies' under the Common Law Constitution," in William N. Eskridge, Jr., and Sanford Levinson, eds., *Constitutional Stupidities, Constitutional Tragedies* (forthcoming, New York University Press).

24. My views on the debate over originalism are described in detail in Earl M. Maltz, *Rethinking Constitutional Law: Originalism, Interventionism, and the Politics of Judicial Review* (Lawrence, Kan., 1994).

CHAPTER EIGHT

Originalism—The Deceptive Evil:
Brown v. Board of Education

WALTER F. MURPHY

Earl Maltz's chapter is both thoughtful and learned. On some specific points I agree with him and on others I disagree. Our most important difference lies in our answers to the question of how to interpret "the constitution"—whatever that term includes—and I concentrate on this single point. Maltz espouses "originalism,"[1] the requirement that interpreters construe "the constitution" as it was supposedly understood[2] by the people who founded the system or amended it.[3] Interpreters, he says, "who are unconstrained by the original understanding will simply constitutionalize the views of the particular segment of the ruling elite from which they are drawn."[4]

The discretion that interpreters have to read their own values into as well as out of the "constitution" has posed a serious problem. The American practice of relegating, despite the ambiguity of the constitutional text, to judges much of the task of constitutional interpretation increases the gravity of the problem for the democratic aspects of constitutional democracy. At the federal level, judges are largely free from the check of the ballot box; and the other limitations on their power, while potentially formidable, are seldom deployed. Thus Maltz's focus on judicial interpretations of "the constitution" is certainly a sensible limitation for one paper, doubly so since his advocacy of originalism occurs within the context of a discussion of *Brown v. Board of Education.*

Judges have often and obviously (critics would add "flagrantly") utilized their interpretive discretion to constitutionalize some controversial public policies as well as to "de-constitutionalize" others. In both operations, they have tried to imprint into the constitutional order equally controversial concepts of what that system is all about. Thus, protests against judge-made constitutional revision have echoed throughout American history from the time of John Jay through Thomas Jefferson, Andrew Jackson, Abraham Lincoln, and Franklin Roosevelt, down to the present day.[3]

Originalism assumes an answer to a fundamental question: What is it that constitutional interpreters should interpret? Replies must fall into one of five categories: (1) the text, the whole text, and nothing but the text; (2) less than the entire text; (3) all of the text plus something else; (4) some of the text plus something else; or (5) something else rather than any of the text. Many commentators and public officials such as Justice Hugo L. Black, who, like Maltz, wish to restrain judicial discretion, have claimed that the sole legitimate subject of constitutional construction is the text itself. Interpreters who add to, subtract from, substitute other writings for, or read economic, political, or moral theories into that document inevitably, however wisely and nobly, change what "We, the people" approved and to which we, including judges, have sworn allegiance.

Despite his purpose of curtailing judicial discretion, Maltz allies himself with those who would give the third answer: "the text plus." His "plus" would be original understanding. This reading turns original understanding into a sprawling superconstitutional text: Its many-colored contents control the meaning of the supposedly authoritative constitutional document. That ordering of authority has huge implications not only for the meaning of the supremacy clause of Article VI but also for the nature of the political system itself.

A question immediately arises: Why should judges look at original understanding of that document at all? To contend that "the constitution" includes the founders' "understandings"—or, to phrase the matter slightly differently, that later interpreters are bound by what the founders "understood" their words to mean— requires justification outside of history. To argue that we are bound by what the founders understood because the founders understood that we would be so bound is to go around in a logical circle. The typical justification is rooted in democratic theory:[6] We the people approved not only the constitutional text but also our understanding of that text and its ramifications.

Alas, the extant historical record leaves grave doubts that the founders of 1787–88 intended their understandings, of which only some of them left hints and most of them not even a single clue that we know of, rather than the document they wrote and ratified, to form authoritative interpretive guides.[7] But even if the founders silently intended their understandings to bind later generations, why are we so bound? Ratifiers voted on the initial document and later on its amendments, not on unknown "understandings" of various drafters and ratifiers. As Justice Felix Frankfurter once noted in discussing the legislative history of the Fourteenth Amendment: In the final analysis, the states ratified the text of the amendment, not the speeches.[8]

A related question arises: Even if "the constitution" includes original understanding of the document as well as the document itself, why should that understanding be uniquely privileged?[9] Why should interpreters not give equal or greater weight to traditions that have since developed? Why not early (or later) interpretations? Why not political theories like democracy and constitutionalism? Why not current conceptions of how best to achieve the text's explicitly stated objectives? An originalist answer would have to run something like this: "Because the founders understood 'the constitution' to exclude these items." To be convincing, that response would have to be accompanied not only by an answer to the earlier question of why such an unstated understanding binds the future, but also by prodigious research demonstrating that the founders actually shared such an understanding.

Maltz's paper does not address these larger issues. He focuses on originalism and restricts himself to one reason—again a fair restriction for one paper—for including and elevating it into "the constitution": It would restrain interpretive, or more particularly judicial, discretion. This objective is worthy, but originalism would both broaden and cloak discretion.

One of Maltz's arguments for originalism's restraining effect on judges is that it steers them into an area where they supposedly have expertise. In effect, his reasoning here is much like Sherlock Holmes's argument from exclusion: If we eliminate the wrong answers, the answer that remains must be correct. Judges seldom have any special training in philosophy, theology, anthropology, or sociology, Maltz contends; yet they often function as if they do. The usual qualifications for a justice, he writes, "are that the nominee be well connected politically; that he or she share the basic political philosophy of the president; and (if the nomination is to be considered a 'good' one), that the person have demonstrated mastery of the art of manipulating technical rules of law. None of these qualifications suggests great insight into questions of morality or public policy."[10] Nor, I must add, do any of these qualifications suggest great ability as an historian. Moreover, we have hard evidence that judges are usually poor historians. They have had no training as historians and, apparently, little aptitude. Professionals make the point ad nauseam that, as historians, judges tend to be sloppy amateurs.[11] "The Court," Leonard W. Levy complained, "rarely gets its history right."[12] Even fellow judges cannot always resist being snide. People who trust the Supreme Court's version of constitutional history, the former Chief Justice of West Virginia remarked, "also probably believe in the Tooth Fairy and the Easter Bunny."[13]

Maltz's logic here is somewhat analogous to that which my sports agent, if I had such an agent and he were a devoutly practicing alcoholic, might make in negotiating with the personnel director of the Green Bay Packers: Murphy is a terrible golfer, he's an awful skater, the only thing he can dribble is food, and he can't hit a curve ball. Therefore you should draft him as a middle linebacker. (My insurance agent would be the first, but surely not the last, to object.)

Historians form a distinct and learned, though imperfect, profession. They need and typically obtain highly specialized training in how (and where) to discover, analyze, and evaluate documentary evidence of the sort that originalism offers as the superconstitutional text. Their objective is, or is supposed to be, truth. Some historians have had personal, ideological, and careerist axes to grind; and, like other human beings, historians can be seduced by fads; but these are failings, betrayals of Clio, and, professionally, mortal sins.[14] In contrast, the objective of attorneys, the people from whom judges are apt to have received most of their professional training and from whom they are now apt to obtain most assistance, is to win a case, to stress what helps their clients, and to downplay or ignore what does not. For law-office history, careful selection of quotations to support clients' causes is the heart of the art. Lawyers are not apt even to know about, much less to have time to explore, unpublished papers squirreled away in archives (and sometimes in attics) around the country.[15]

It could happen, of course, that amateur historians competing in an adversary system would produce the raw materials from which judges could discern the past; but the probabilities of that leading to the discovery of truth would be enormously increased if judges had the technical expertise to assess the probative value of the competing research, both as to which materials were included and which ones were omitted. But no professional historian has yet graced the Supreme Court's bench.

In earlier writings,[16] I attacked originalism for two basic reasons. First, as a matter of constitutional policy: If originalism did function as it is supposed to, it would restrain not merely judges but the entire nation in coping with constitutional problems that the founders, despite their wisdom, did not foresee. To respond that, when the nation encounters such problems people need only amend the constitutional text, presumes those problems will allow the complexities of the amending process to unfold without grievous harm to the system. Moreover, if successfully and frequently used, the constitutional document would, as John Marshall warned, "partake of a prolixity of a legal code, and could scarcely be embraced by the human mind."[17] It may be more prudent for an originalist to respond that the text's words are sufficiently open-ended to allow the nation to cope with whatever crises arise; but that answer opens wide the doors to interpretive discretion. Thus we arrive either at crises that might threaten grave national injury or change the nature of the constitutional document, or we affirm the necessity of spacious interpretive discretion, precisely what originalism was supposed to eliminate.

My second line of attack concerned the historical record. Historians agree that the Federalists, though not the Anti-Federalists, wanted to construct a stronger central government, to leave considerable but restricted authority with the states, and, by accomplishing these twin tasks, to enhance the liberty of individual citizens. But once we go beyond those sorts of general statements about the Federalists, we glide on thin evidentiary ice. The initial problem is linguistic. By the time of the Revolution, American and British English had diverged in significant ways. And, although there were several early dictionaries of American English—e.g., Caleb Alexander, *The Columbian Dictionary of the English Language* (1800)—the first comprehensive work, *The American Dictionary of the English Language*, was not published until 1828, forty years after adoption of the constitutional document and thirty-seven years after ratification of the Bill of Rights. Moreover, the compiler was Noah Webster, a sturdy Federalist, who set for himself the dual task of instructing his readers in matters political as well as definitional.[18]

The one originalist with whose writings I am familiar who tried to address linguistic difficulties was William W. Crosskey.[19] His three volumes were sharply contentious, arguing that all of American constitutional history was wrongly understood: The founders had tried to establish a unitary state, with the former colonies relegated to serving as mustering areas for militia and electoral districts for representatives. His work was just as sharply contested; indeed, it spawned a cottage industry of attacks. Nevertheless, Crosskey faced up to the harsh fact that originalists who take their originalism seriously must reconstruct a dictionary of American English of the 1780s relevant to the constitutional text.

Less dedicated originalists might choose to ignore linguistic differences and use a more or less contemporary dictionary of British English, such as Dr. Samuel Johnson's, as a rough approximation. Alternatively, as most originalists do, they might simply pretend that current English serves as an adequate approximation for the English of the late eighteenth century. Rough approximations, however, seldom yield answers precise enough to settle important disputes about constitutional meaning. Originalists might also rely on Sir William Blackstone's *Commentaries on the Laws of England, Coke on Littleton,* or one of several other treatises widely read by American lawyers of the day. Still, it is not manifest that the founders wished to adopt the British common law in its entirety. More serious is the fact that most originalists anchor their claims in democratic theory and so would have to root "the constitution" in the American population as a whole, not merely in lawyers. And Blackstone and Coke were not everyday reading in the colonies.

Even if we assume that we can read eighteenth-century language as eighteenth-century citizens did and could also insulate ourselves from the subconscious effects of our knowledge of how constitutional tragedies like the Civil War were affected by constitutional interpretation, we would still be left with immense documentary difficulties. As Justice Robert H. Jackson once said, the materials from which interpreters are supposed to divine original understanding are "almost as enigmatic as the dreams that Joseph was called upon to interpret for Pharaoh."[20]

There was no stenographer present at Philadelphia; the secretary's minutes were a shambles, and no delegate whose work has survived utilized anything like a modern system of shorthand. Several delegates jotted down notes, but at least one set, that of Robert Yates of New York, seems to have been an elaborate forgery written by Citizen Genet—he of earlier diplomatic fame.[21] Madison took the most extensive notes available to us. But, although he obtained manuscripts from some of the other delegates, he wrote many of his synopses in longhand while actively participating in debate himself. (He claimed not to have spoken from a prepared manuscript himself, yet he included long quotations from his own speeches.) Furthermore, for several months after the Convention adjourned, he continued to edit what he had written, even doing touch-up work some years later. And those notes are merely notes. Students can enact a moot convention, with each playing the role of a framer, and read out loud all of Madison's summaries of each day's "speeches" in an hour, about one-sixth of the time it took the delegates to deliver the unedited versions.

Available records of debates on ratification paint a richer portrait. We have wonderful collections of the arguments on all sides in the campaigns that led to the election of delegates to the state conventions.[22] Publius, Brutus, and hundreds of others displayed an intellectual splendor that Americans of the turn of the twenty-first century can only envy: not thirty-second "sound bites," but serious, reasoned debates conducted in newspapers, pamphlets, and public meetings. These discussions were full, nuanced, and carried on in writings as well as speeches.

On the other hand, accounts of what went on in the ratifying conventions are problematic. Official stenographers were present but they were not skilled in shorthand. Worse, as in Massachusetts, they were sometimes partisans who felt small duty to report debates accurately. John Marshall, a delegate to Virginia's convention, allegedly complained that "if my name had not been prefixed to the speaches [sic] I would never have recognized them as productions of mine."[23] In 1827, Jonathan Elliot published the first of eight (or more) editions of a four-volume collection of what purported to be the speeches given there;[24] unfortunately, connections between what Elliot reports and what was said in the conventions are tenuous at best. Although he himself admitted that "the sentiments they contain may, in some instances, have been inaccurately taken down, and, in others, probably too faintly sketched fully to gratify the inquisitive politician," he believed they "may form an excellent guide in expounding many doubtful points in that [constitutional] instrument."[25] Painstaking research by Jensen, Kaminski, and Saldino[26] has diminished but not removed our ignorance. As with Philadelphia, we know the state conventions ratified the text but precious little else of interpretive value.

This state of the historical record allows originalists vast scope for discretion. We have little knowledge, and are not apt to gain more, about how most of the men at Philadelphia and the state capitals understood various clauses of the constitutional text beyond the fact that ultimately, and sometimes reluctantly, a majority of them approved the document as a whole. If we restrict ourselves to the understandings of important men, we face fewer but still huge problems. After ratification, even Madison and Hamilton sometimes changed their minds about how they understood the new document. More telling to advocates of democratic theory would be that much hard evidence would be needed to equate the views of a few prominent, however brilliant, men with those either of an entire generation or of the elected representatives of that generation.

The views of the senators and representatives in the Congress that proposed the Fourteenth Amendment are less unclear but hardly clear. We do have the *Congressional Globe* with the debates recorded by shorthand stenographers, though the almost perfect grammar of the speeches raises questions about how much editing was done. In any event, *The Globe*'s pages show wide substantive disagreement among the speakers; it also shows that a majority of men in both houses did not speak about the proposal at all. I have too often sat mutely in faculty meetings when colleagues who were on my side blabbed arrant nonsense to believe that silence connotes agreement with a speaker. The situation in the state legislatures was even murkier than for the ratifying conventions. Only a few states kept detailed accounts of their legislative debates; and, while we have some newspaper coverage, journalists appeared less interested in the process than their predecessors had been in 1787–88. Furthermore, the published stories report diverse understandings of what lawmakers thought they were approving or disapproving.

Thus even the most conscientious originalists must exercise considerable creative imagination in surmising the mental images that danced in the minds of long dead—and often quiet—founders. I have argued that constitutional interpretation necessarily involves both discretion and creativity. Therefore, my quarrel with originalism lies elsewhere: in its claims to provide a set of objectively discoverable interpretive standards and to narrow interpreters' discretion. In fact, while pretending to do both, it does neither.

My third line of attack is related to the second. The very term "original understanding" begs a critical question: Was there in 1787–88 or 1866–68 or during debates about other constitutional amendments one and only one understanding of what was being discussed? The recent history of the women's rights amendment should give originalists pause. If there had been anything like agreement on what that proposal entailed, it probably would have been rather promptly voted up or down. Any fair-minded person who reads the pamphlets for and against the constitutional text of 1787 would see an even more complicated situation.

Writing before scholars has brought together so many of the relevant documents, Joseph Story said that "there can be no certainty, either that the different state conventions in ratifying the constitution, gave the same uniform interpretation to its language, or that, even in a single state convention, the same reasoning prevailed with a majority, much less the whole of the supporters of it."[27] Later research has demonstrated what Story suspected: The founders did not debate a single constitutional text, or even two documents; what writings we have show they disagreed not only about the problems to be solved and how to solve them, but also about what the new text meant. There were several original understandings, not one; I would estimate at least three and possibly as many as a dozen.

Let us take an issue central for most orginalists, the scope of the judicial power to interpret "the constitution." Hamilton's assertions of a modest role in *Federalist* No. 78 are familiar. Less familiar are the Anti-Federalist essays of Brutus (quite possibly the pen name of Robert Yates) to which Hamilton was replying:

> The judicial are not only to decide questions arising upon the meaning of the constitution in law, but also in equity. By this they are empowered, to explain the constitution according to the reasoning spirit of it, without being confined to the words or letter. . . .
>
> They [federal judges] will give the sense of every article of the constitution, that may from time to time come before them. And in their decisions they will not confine themselves to any fixed or established rules, but will determine, according to what appears to them, the reason and spirit of the constitution. The opinions of the supreme court, whatever they may be, will have the force of law; because there is no power provided in the constitution, that can correct their errors, or control their adjudications. From this court there is no appeal. And I conceive the legislature themselves,

cannot set aside a judgment of this court, because they are authorized by the constitution to decide in the last resort. The legislature
must be controlled by the constitution, and not the constitution by
them. They have therefore no more right to set aside any judgment
pronounced upon the construction of the constitution, than they
have to take from the president, the chief command of the army
and navy, and commit it to some other person. The reason is plain;
the judicial and executive derive their authority from the same
source, that the legislature do theirs. . . .

Here as elsewhere, we must choose between competing understandings and we must give reasons for our choices. How do we
choose between Hamilton's prayer for judicial modesty and Brutus's predictions of expansive judicial discretion? First, we might
say that Hamilton's side won the debate: Eventually all thirteen
states ratified the next text. True, but did the voters and ratifiers
do so because they believed Publius rather than Brutus? On that
score we have no evidence. And we do have contemporary evidence that the issue can be complicated. Many of us who support
heavy taxation of cigarettes do so in the prayerful hope that the
tobacco companies are correct in claiming that such levies will
bankrupt them. Furthermore, it is questionable how many ratifiers were aware of, much less believers in, either gospel. Both
men wrote for the people of New York; and when No. 78 was published, eight states had already ratified.

A second originalist argument might be that Hamilton had
been at the Philadelphia Convention and he should have known
at least how the delegates there understood the text. But Yates, if,
indeed, he were Brutus, had also been at Philadelphia. Most important, both men had been absent when what became Article III
was debated and crafted.

A third argument might be that history has vindicated Hamilton, not Brutus. But no sophisticated originalist would make that
argument directly, for it would imply that we have not had a serious problem with judicial discretion. A stronger argument would
be: History as a moving picture be damned, history as a snapshot
is what counts; and Hamilton's words captured the general under-

standing of 1787–88. Perhaps Hamilton did, perhaps he did not. What is the evidence for either side? In 1787–88 most Federalists were not foes of judicial power.

Disagreements like that between Publius and Brutus force interpreters, be they appointed judges, elected officials, academic commentators, or private citizens, to choose. And if constitutional government establishes, as commentators as distant from each other in time and ideology as Noah Webster and Ronald Dworkin assert, an "empire of reason," interpreters must give reasons for their choices among competing understandings. They cannot merely say, "The founders understood the text to mean _____," and cite a speech or two. Undoubtedly some founders did so understand the text; and just as surely other founders did not. Originalists who remain consistent with their principles must explain why they accept as authoritative one set of founders over others. And simply demonstrating, as they may, that one set made more cogent arguments will not do. A consistent originalist does not accept original understanding because it was good, prudent, or beautiful; a consistent originalist accepts original understanding even if it is evil, foolish, or ugly.[28] What supposedly gives original understanding authority is that, with whatever warts, it is the understanding of the founding generation.

One line of retreat for originalists would be to claim that the true test of initial understanding would be the way in which judges interpreted the text early on. For the text of 1787–88, that retreat quickly turns into a rout. First of all, we would need reasons how and why "judges" should become a surrogate for "the people" and/or how nonelected judges can read the public mind, especially in the absence of a reliable written record to interpret. If we merely concede that such a judicial role was understood at the beginning, we must also accept something akin to Brutus's description of judicial preeminence in the new constitutional order. At that point, concerns about judicial discretion and, more particularly, judicial activism become heretical for originalists, unless they can show that later amendments were understood to impose general restrictions on the judiciary's interpretive ambit.

And that task is impossible. Nonoriginalists can readily concede that the Eleventh Amendment was designed to undo *Chis-
holm v. Georgia*, the "citizenship clause" of the Fourteenth Amendment to erase *Dred Scott*'s[29] reading of the document, the Six-
teenth the narrow construction of the *Income Tax Cases*,[30] and the
Twenty-sixth *Oregon v. Mitchell*'s[31] interpretation. None of these
amendments, however, purported to restrict the judiciary's basic
interpretive power; and I am not aware of any serious historian's
claiming otherwise. Even the Fourteenth Amendment, which explicitly broadened congressional power, increased judicial power,
for Congress quickly enacted statutes that pretty much turned all
the matters of Section 1 over to federal judges.

Assuming clever originalists could get themselves out of this
logical dilemma, they would be trapped by a familiar problem:
Early judges disagreed with one another about such fundamental
issues as the reach of judicial power. In *Calder v. Bull* (1798), the
first serious judicial debate on the legitimate scope of the Court's
constitutional interpretation, Justice Samuel Chase wrote:

> I cannot subscribe to the omnipotence of a state legislature, or that
> it is absolute and without controul; although its authority should
> not be expressly restrained by the constitution, or fundamental law
> of the state. The people of the United States erected their constitu-
> tions or forms of government, to establish justice, to promote the
> general welfare, to secure the blessings of liberty, and to protect
> their persons and property from violence. The purposes for which
> men enter into society will determine the nature and terms of the
> social compact; and as they are the foundation of the legislative
> power, they will decide what are the proper objects of it. This funda-
> mental principle flows from the very nature of our free republican
> governments. . . . There are acts which the federal or state legisla-
> tures cannot do, without exceeding their authority. There are cer-
> tain vital principles in our free republican governments which will
> determine and overrule an apparent and flagrant abuse of legisla-
> tive power; as to authorize manifest injustice by positive law. . . . An
> act of the legislature (for I cannot call it a law), contrary to the great
> first principles of the social compact, cannot be considered a right-

ful exercise of legislative authority. The obligation of a law in governments established on express compact, and on republican principles, must be determined by the nature of the power on which it is founded.

Justice James Iredell disagreed:

> If . . . the legislature of the Union, or the legislature of any member of the Union, shall pass a law within the general scope of their constitutional power, the court cannot pronounce it to be void, merely because it is, in their judgment, contrary to the principles of natural justice. The ideas of natural justice are regulated by no fixed standard . . . all that the court could properly say . . . would be that the legislature (possessed of an equal right of opinion) had passed an act which, in the opinion of the judges, was inconsistent with the abstract principles of natural justice. There are then but two lights, in which the subject can be viewed: 1st. If the legislature pursue the authority delegated to them, their acts are valid. 2d. If they transgress the boundaries of that authority, their acts are invalid. In the former case, they exercise the discretion vested in them by the people, to whom alone they are responsible for the faithful discharge of their trust: but in the latter case, they violate a fundamental law, which must be our guide, whenever we are called upon as judges, to determine the validity of a legislative act.

Chase's ideas were nearer to those of Brutus than of Hamilton. Iredell proposed a much different and narrower normative concept of judicial authority, a positivistic view rather close to Hamilton's. My point is not that either Chase or Iredell had the better of the debate.[32] My point is simpler and more basic: Once again, to justify choosing sides here, originalists must provide reasons, reasons that transcend originalism, for available historical evidence of the understandings of both founders and early judges provides diametrically opposed answers.

Earl Maltz is aware of the kinds of criticisms I have lodged, and he concedes the necessity for originalists' developing "supplemental evidentiary rules" to guide interpreters where history "is unclear or reveals disagreements among the framers."[33] This task is as daunting as it is essential, for in many (most?) critical places the evidence is both unclear and ambiguous. To my knowledge, Maltz has not yet published those supplementary rules, and I confess to being baffled as to how such rules might read if they are to be workable and still channel choice. I can envision such rules if we restrict original understanding to what Ronald Dworkin calls conceptions rather than concepts, but then no constitutional text could survive for more than a generation. Thomas Jefferson would have applauded that lifespan, but the founding generation explicitly rejected the notion of a proper time limit. Thus this version of the new rules would violate a categoric original choice, which should certainly offend originalists.

A version of the new rules that, where the record is unclear on points in several directions, would purport to help interpreters divine what the founders understood by the concepts they wrote and a different set of founders ratified would either be mystical formulations to validate personal choices or admissions of the legitimacy of much of the constitutional interpretation against which originalists protest. In constrast, what judges like William J. Brennan, Jr., claim to do is quite straightforward: to apply the founders' general purposes, as stated in the document, to current problems.

I do not imply that conscientious constitutional interpreters should ignore the founders of 1787–88, early (or later) interpreters, or emenders.[34] A prudent modern interpreter should be attentive to what people as astute as Madison, Hamilton, Brutus, Jefferson, or Marshall thought about the constitutional order they were trying to confect. These men were intelligent, experienced, and dedicated; we are deeply indebted to them and owe it to ourselves—not to them—to consult their wisdom. But, as Justice Benjamin Cardozo wrote to his brethren in 1934: The founders "did not see the changes in the relation between states and nation or in the play of social forces that lay hidden in the womb of time. . . . Their beliefs to be significant must be adjusted to the world they knew."[35] As Charles P. Curtis noted a half-century ago, what the founders said, they said; what they did not say, they left to us.[36]

And they did not say "interpret 'the constitution' as we understand it." Indeed, they could not have so said, at least with any truth or conviction, for they had many different understandings.

Constitutional interpretation inevitably entails discretion; it inevitably entails creativity. Discretion and creativity pose dangers, but we cannot keep either in check by pretending to read the minds of dead men. When alive, these men probably never thought about many of those problems and, if they did, left us scant evidence of what those thoughts were. We know the purposes the founders endorsed: The Preamble states them elegantly and succinctly. The rest of the text outlines the structures they established to cope with problems and sketches the rights they meant to hallow, including others unlisted but still reserved to the people. That constitutional text has worked upon and has been worked upon by generations of citizens; these interactions have created a constitutional order and a constitutional culture that transcend the imaginations of even the most dazzling of the founders. Interpreters must construe the amended text as it exists within that order and culture, not as in mental images that may or may not have been in the founders' minds.

NOTES

1. For a fuller exposition of his theory of originalism, see Earl Maltz, *Rethinking Constitutional Law: Originalism, Interventionism, and the Politics of Judicial Review* (Lawrence: University of Kansas Press, 1994).

2. Deserving of an article of its own is an analysis of the implications of and the reasons behind originalists' changes in terminology in recent decades. At one time, they sought "original intent." This search involved many difficulties, not the least of which was distinguishing between "intent," what the framers (usually not the ratifiers) meant to mean, and "purpose," their larger objectives. Few interpreters would deny seeking the latter. For many reasons and mostly, I believe, because of the influence of Justice Antonin Scalia, originalists now seek "original understanding," the meaning that the founding (or emending) generation would have put on the clauses of the constitutional text. Unaddressed, as

far as I can determine, are the problems of the extent to which understandings of specific clauses can be reconciled with understanding the document as a whole and how a quest for general understanding (if there were one) can be differentiated from a search for purpose. Identification of the two would again threaten to fold originalism into the interpretive theories of its opponents, such as the late Justice William J. Brennan, Jr.: "The Constitution of the United States: Contemporary Ratification," 27 *So. Tex.* L.J. 433 (1986); reprinted in large part in Walter F. Murphy, James E. Fleming, and Sotirios A. Barber, *American Constitutional Interpretation* (2d ed.; Westbury, NY: Foundation Press, 1995), 236–42.

3. In the version of the chapter I read, Maltz uses the word "framers." I infer that he includes not only the men at Philadelphia but those who campaigned for and against delegates to the state conventions and, most especially, the delegates themselves. An inference of this sort is not only fair, but necessary. In *Rethinking Constitutional Law,* he finds the source of the text's legitimacy in ratification, though he contends that ratification was done by states, not by the people of the several states. He accepts the logical conclusion that the document is a compact among the states (32). By analogy, I infer that Maltz includes ratifiers of the various amendments, not merely those in Congress who spoke and voted for or against the proposed changes to the text. I confess, however, that I could only guess what Congress's forcing the southern states to ratify the Fourteenth Amendment does to his theory of the constitution as a compact among states. Perhaps he believes that the fiction that such force did not occur was part of the understanding of the amendment's ratification and thus takes precedence over historical reality. Alternatively, he may believe the Fourteenth Amendment is not included in the valid constitutional text, an interesting though hardly novel thesis, which would make the compact theory more plausible as well as invalidate the Fourteenth Amendment and *Brown v. Board.*

4. See p. 150. In context this statement supposedly explains how the votes in *Shaw v. Reno* reflected the ideology of various presidents and their parties. All members of the majority were nominated (Maltz says "appointed," but Robert H. Bork, Douglas H. Ginsburg, Anthony M. Kennedy, and even William H. Rehnquist might insist that the Senate played a role here) by either Ronald Reagan or George Bush, while "three of the four dissenters—Byron R. White, Harry A. Blackmun, and John Paul Stevens—were selected by other presidents." Indeed, they

were: John F. Kennedy, most assuredly a liberal, nominated White; Richard M. Nixon, hardly a paragon of liberalism, chose Blackmun; Nixon's conservative Republican successor in office Gerald Ford selected Stevens; and Bush, who abhorred the L word, nominated the fourth dissenter, David Souter. Thus it turns out that the president's party and ideology explains little, if anything, about the division in *Shaw.* One Democratic nominee dissented along with three conservative Republican choices against the views of judges selected by other conservative Republicans. Without doubt, ideology enters into judicial decision making, but hardly in such a simplistic way.

5. Indeed, the current term, "judicial activism," is bandied about so much that it often implies no more than that the speaker disagrees with judges about the meaning of the constitutional text or of a statute. Insofar as Maltz's discussion would restrict that term, it would be to apply it to judges who did not follow originalism.

6. There is a nice touch of irony here. Many Anti-Federalists made the point, probably correct, that few Federalist leaders were good democrats and that the new text was un- if not anti-democratic. Many originalists and nonoriginalists alike confuse "government by consent" with democratic government. The document of 1787 was surely not democratic; some amendments have made it more so. But the real changes have come through formal (one person, one vote) and informal constitutional interpretation.

7. See especially H. Jefferson Powell, "The Original Understanding of Original Intent," 98 *Harv. L. Rev.* 885 (1985); and the response by Charles A. Lofgren, "Original Understanding of Original Intent," 5 *Con'l Comm.* 77 (1988).

8. Adamson v. California, 332 U.S. 46, concur. op., 64 (1947).

9. In fact, of course, many liberal and conservative interpreters, including judges, do not restrict their constitutional editing to originalism. Justice Black saw no contradiction in simultaneously espousing originalism and pure textualism while reading democratic theory into the document. Justice Antonin Scalia, the leading judicial apostle of originalism, also reads democratic theory into the "constitution," even as he decries others' efforts to use political theory in constitutional interpretation.

10. See p. 117.

11. See, e.g., Alfred H. Kelly, "Clio and the Court: An Illicit Love Affair," 1965 *Sup. Ct. Rev.* 119; Leonard W. Levy, *Original Intent and the Framers' Constitution* (New York: Macmillan, 1988), esp. chap. 14;

Charles A. Miller, *The Supreme Court and the Uses of History* (Cambridge, Mass.: Harvard University Press, 1969); Paul Murphy, "A Time to Reclaim: The Current Challenge of American Constitutional History," 69 *Am. Hist. Rev.* 64 (1963).

12. Levy, *Original Intent*, 320.

13. Richard Neely, *How Courts Govern America* (New Haven: Yale University Press, 1981), p. 18.

14. Which is not say that they will be punished during this accounting period.

15. It is ironic that Robert H. Bork's panegyric to originalism depends almost entirely on judicial opinions and other secondary sources for its argument from history. See *The Tempting of America: The Political Seduction of the Law* (New York: Free Press, 1990).

16. "The Constitution: Interpretation and Intent," 45 *A.B.A.J.* 592 (1959); "Constitutional Interpretation: The Art of the Historian, Magician, or Statesman?" 87 *Yale L. J.* 1752 (1978); Murphy, Fleming, and Barber, *American Constitutional Interpretation*, pp. 389–93.

17. M'Culloch v. Maryland, 4 Wh. 316, 407 (1819).

18. See Noah Webster, *Collection of Essays and Fugitive Writings on Moral, Historical, Political and Literary Subjects* (1790); and, more generally, David Simpson, *The Politics of American English, 1776–1850* (New York: Oxford University Press, 1986), esp. chap. 2.

19. *Politics and the Constitution* (Chicago: University of Chicago Press, 1953, 2 vols.); long after Crosskey's death, William Jeffrey, Jr,. edited a third volume (Chicago: University of Chicago Press, 1980). These books grew out of a law review article that Crosskey began to write in 1937, attacking the Old Court's mangling of the New Deal. The Court did so, he believed, because the justices did not understand the language of the constitutional document. Among the many reviewers who engaged Crosskey on the accuracy of his definitions was Henry M. Hart, Jr., "Professor Crosskey and Judicial Review," 67 *Harv. L. Rev.* 1456 (1954).

20. Youngstown Sheet & Tube Co. v. Sawyer, 343 U.S. 579, 634, concur. op. (1952). For a succinct analysis of these difficulties, see James H. Hutson, "The Creation of the Constitution: The Integrity of the Documentary Record," 65 *Tex. L. Rev.* 1 (1986). A distinguished historian, Hutson is also chief of the Manuscript Division of the Library of Congress.

21. See Hutson, "Creation of the Constitution," 9ff.

22. In 1976, Merrill Jensen and his associates began a massive project to construct a documentary record of the ratifying process. They have

put together different accounts of what was said in the conventions, and, equally or even more helpful, to assemble many of the contemporary documents circulated during the campaigns to choose delegates. Later John P. Kaminski and Gaspare J. Saldino took over as general editors. As of December 1994, volumes 1–3, 8–10, and 13–16 had appeared. See *The Documentary History of the Ratification of the Constitution* (Madison: University of Wisconsin Press, 1976—). Among the more useful collection of documents for the Bill of Rights are Helen E. Veit and Kenneth E. Bowling, eds., *Creating the Bill of Rights: The Documentary Record from the First Federal Congress* (Baltimore: Johns Hopkins University Press, 1981); and Bernard Schwartz, ed., *The Bill of Rights* (New York: Chelsea House, 1971), 2 vols.

23. Herbert A. Johnson, ed., *The Papers of John Marshall* (Chapel Hill: University of North Carolina Press, 1974), I, 256n.7, bases this quotation on a memorandum by Thomas H. Bayly of a conversation with Marshall in 1832.

24. *The Debates in the Several State Conventions on the Adoption of the Federal Constitution.* I have used the second edition (Washington, D.C.: Printed by and for the Editor, 1836).

25. "Preface to the First Edition," reprinted in ibid., I, v.

26. *The Documentary History of the Ratification of the Constitution.*

27. *Commentaries on the Constitution of the United States* (1st ed.; Boston: Hilliard, Gray, 1833), I, 388–89.

28. What Justice Scalia, the most prominent originalist, loses in consistency, he gains in integrity and courage in his admissions that there are limits to his originalism. See his "Originalism: The Lesser Evil," 57 *U. Cinn. L. Rev.* 849 (1989), reprinted in large part in Murphy, Fleming, and Barber, *American Constitutional Interpretation.* 231–36.

29. 19 How. 393 (1857).

30. Pollock v. Farmers' Loan & Trust, 158 U.S. 691 (1895).

31. 400 U.S. 112 (1970).

32. For a discussion of two early cases decided by the Supreme Court of New Jersey, in which the justices, like Chase, went beyond the text of the constitution, see Wayne D. Moore, "Written and Unwritten Constitutional Law in the Founding Period: The Early New Jersey Cases," 7 *Con'l Comm.* 341 (1990).

33. *Rethinking Constitutional Law, 22.*

34. I do not think it unjust to say that, except on the issue of slavery, the men who framed and ratified the Fourteenth Amendment were not the intellectual equals of the giants of 1787–88.

35. Unpublished concur. op. in Home Building & Loan Ass'n v. Blais-dell, 290 U.S. 398 (1934), in the Papers of Harlan Fiske Stone, Library of Congress; reprinted in Murphy, Fleming, and Barber, *American Constitutional Interpretation*, 211ff.

36. *Lions under the Throne* (Boston: Houghton Mifflin, 1947), 7–8.

CHAPTER NINE

Roe v. Wade: Speaking the Unspeakable

JEAN BETHKE ELSHTAIN

HERE IS THE CRUX of the matter. There is no denying that, with conception, a life process that is undeniably human has begun. What is the moral status of that nascent life? When is he or she— for we are always talking about a concrete being—fully enveloped by the moral community: at conception, at some point during pregnancy, or at the moment of birth? Reflect, if you will, on whether or not you experience any moral squeamishness in connection with abortion and at what stage. That squeamishness is an important sign of our sense that a life process worthy of human dignity is at stake. I believe we should respect that moral sense. That is the first card I will put on the table.

The second is political. I think the Supreme Court decision in *Roe v. Wade* launched a civic debacle. Why is that? Precisely because there was promising *political* discourse going on in many states in 1973. The negation of those messy (because they were political) processes in such a decisive matter polarized our society in ways that might have been avoided. Sometimes polarization cannot be avoided. Sometimes an absolutely clear moral and political imprimatur is at stake. I take that to be the case, for example, in *Brown v. Board of Education.*[1] But *Roe v. Wade* is a different story. The pattern of legislative compromise and revision going on in many states at the time the decision was handed down demonstrates this quite clearly, I will have more to say on this matter.

My practical suggestion, in light of the two cards I have thus far put into play, is not so startling. I believe that we should regulate abortion in ways that circumscribe a "freedom" that is at best

175

chimerical, especially for women. The present "freedom," for example, presents a great burden for women who are told that they alone have the power to choose whether or not to have a child and that they alone are expected to bear the consequences if they do not choose to do so. I suggest we start by disallowing partial birth abortion, a move favored by a wide majority of the American population at present and a procedure that the American Obstetrics and Gynecological Association claims is "required" in so few situations that the need for it is almost nonexistent. Partial birth abortion is a repellent, barbaric deed that should not hide behind the cloak of law in a minimally decent society. I would next move to disallow sex selection as the basis for abortion: gender prejudice does not deserve the sanction of law. Again, the vast majority of Americans agree, save for a small number of pro-abortion absolutists. Then we might move on to further attempts at social dialogue. The goal is to agree on certain restrictions—that a workable agreement is already in place on partial-birth abortion and sex selection—and go on from there. The goal is to keep alive social civility in a pluralistic society as we keep alive more humans-in-formation.

So, my cards are on the table. Below I will unpack the dialogic encounter by which I arrived at this position. But, for just a moment, let's think about the decision itself. One can disagree with the reasonning in *Roe*, which many do, finding it a badly argued case at best, and still agree with the outcome. I disagree with both argument and outcome. The Court itself is struggling to find some middle ground, having recognized that *Roe* is flawed. Bear in mind why this is such a fraught matter. Abortion is a process that involves a direct physical assault on an embryo or fetus: it is not simply failure to aid. And there is no moral consensus— none—as to whether this is ever permissible and, if so, when and under what sorts of exigent circumstances. The Court in *Roe* bypassed these concerns, treating them with little of the gravitas they deserve.

What was up for the Court to decide in *Roe*? It was presented with a Texas statute that made it a crime to procure an abortion unless the life of the mother was threatened.[2] The brief filed in behalf of the litigant claimed that this violated the due process clause of the Fourteenth Amendment, among other things, by overriding her right of privacy—a right the Court had enshrined in various "penumbras" surrounding the Due Process Clause and the Bill of Rights.[3] The litigant, it followed, had both a privacy and a liberty interest in overturning any restrictive abortion statute.

In its decision written by Justice Harry Blackmun and handed down on January 22, 1973, the Court placed enormous power in the hands of medical practitioners by setting up a trimester-based test that greatly limited the power of states to regulate abortion. According to the Court, the relevant decision maker where abortion was concerned in the first trimester was either the woman alone or "her responsible physician." And the grounds for abortion could be pretty much anything from direct harm to psychological distress to a declared "unwanted" pregnancy.

The Court permitted states to regulate in ways "reasonably related" to maternal health in the second semester but those were reduced to the vanishing point in practice. In the third trimester, states could regulate except when an abortion was needed to "preserve the life or health" of the mother. But because health was defined so vaguely, this, too, pretty much set up an unlimited abortion right—this despite the fact that the Court declared that the state does have an interest in fetal life that expands as the pregnancy itself progresses. But this interest is subordinated to the liberty interest infused in the abortion right.[4] By 1990, with the *Webster* case, the Court began to question its own trimester framework by upholding a statute that held that if a woman had reason to believe she was twenty or more weeks pregnant, a physical should determine whether the unborn child was viable. The 1992 *Planned Parenthood v. Casey* decision guaranteed the right to abortion and located constitutional protection in the right to liberty entailed by due process: so state interest and the woman's right created by *Roe* remain on a collision course.

In the eyes of critics, what Justice Blackmun did in *Roe* was to set the court up as a kind of superlegislature by authoring a federal abortion statute where before there had been a mix of state statutes: this by contrast to *Brown v. Board,* which left states enormous leeway in implementing desegregation. That is, in *Brown*, the Court did not design the remedy itself; but in *Roe* it did, thereby eliminating what might be called a *dialogue* with legislatures. Between 1967 and 1973, some nineteen states had passed liberalizing abortion statutes. The Court might have struck down the Texas statute and remanded the matter for further action to the states.[5] This it did not do. We know the travail that resulted.

How, then, to work our way back to a less extreme position than the one encoded in *Roe*? How does one speak about abortion in the wider context of American culture at century's end? For abortion is not a narrowly legal matter: it is about who we are as a people and how we think about who is in and who is out of the moral community. What follows is a dialogue with an imagined interlocutor who, at times, was a voice of objection and resistance to my own position that I believe I not only must take seriously but that I was even prepared to argue for myself twenty-five years ago. For one position does not derive a priori; rather, it was arrived at through contestation, through a combination of moral imperatives and tough political realities. This is the way political theorists, of whom I am one, by contrast to legal scholars—or most legal scholars, anyway—work.

Consider a world in which there are no more births. In her extraordinary novel, *The Children of Men*, P. D. James describes a forlorn globe. The novel is set in Britain in the year 2021. No children have been born—none at all—on planet Earth since the year 1995. The reason for this is not the perfection of a draconian abortion regime but because in that year, for reasons no one understands, all males became infertile. The human race, quite literally, is dying. People are despondent, chagrined, violent. "Western science had been our god," writes the protagonist, one Theodore Faron, an Oxford historian and a cousin to the dictator of Great Britain. He "shares the illusionment" of one whose god has died. Now, overtaken by a "universal negativism," the human race lurches toward its certain demise. Because there will be no future, "all pleasures of the mind and senses sometimes seem . . . no more than pathetic and crumbling defences shored up against our ruin."

Children's playgrounds are dismantled. People disown commitments and responsibilities to, and for, one another except for whatever serves some immediate purpose, what is chosen—what I want—by contrast to what is given. A cult of pseudobirths emerges as women take broken dolls and even baby kittens to be baptized in pseudoceremonies, surreptitiously, for religion, except for a cult of state worship, is forbidden. People thought they had eliminated evil, Faron notes, and all churches in the 1990s moved "from the theology of sin and redemption" to a "sentimental humanism." In the name of compassion, the elderly, no longer needed or wanted, are conducted to a state-sponsored ceremony of coerced (though apparently voluntary) group suicide called the Quietus. Faron concludes that we are "diminished," we humans, if we live without knowledge of the past and without hope of the future. The old prayer, 'That I may see 'my children's children and peace upon Israel,' is no more, and without the possibility of that prayer and the delicate entanglement of all our lives with such fructifying possibility, the world, quite literally, ceases to be. For in a world with no future, a "culture of death," in the words of Pope John Paul II, a world barren and forlorn, a world in which birth has ceased and death is managed and staged, "the very words 'justice,' 'compassion,' 'society,' 'struggle,' 'evil,' would be unheard echoes on an empty air."

We are not there yet. But we may be uncomfortably close.

"Come now, Professor Elshtain, surely you go too far! This vision you and P. D. James appear to share—and the pope, too—is grand, yes, but it is morbid and extreme. There have always been troubles. There has always been killing. Why do you even suspect we are on a trajectory to a secular version of perdition. I cannot share this picture. In fact, given technological advance, the globalization of market forces, the spread of democracy—which you profess to endorse, at least the democracy part—we have a fighting chance for a much better world in the twenty-first century. Why this doom and gloom?"

"Friend, I cannot share your optimism. Why is it that teleological optimists, of whom you seem to be one, always look at the

179

bright side only and refuse to consider the dark undercurrents flowing through late modernity, resolutely averting their eyes from what Reinhold Niebuhr called the ironies of history. The signs of the time are all around us and many are not good."

"Well, if things are so bad and abortion is one of the negative 'signs of the time,' why haven't you written more directly on this matter? I haven't seen you at the forefront of this debate. In fact, I believe you have been quoted in print to the effect that you consider yourself 'moderately pro-life' and, moreover, that you would 'not criticize a woman who chooses abortion.' Are you changing your tune?"

"I know it is tedious when a person claims to have been misquoted. But, as is often the case, important nuances are missed when one goes public about such a controversial matter. I never claimed to be 'moderately pro life.' Instead, I made a political point. My argument was that, given the array of options now before us, I was a 'pro-life moderate.' There is a difference and I will try to articulate it as I go along. I also said that I would not 'condemn' a woman who has an abortion—quite different from 'not criticizing.' I would, in fact, criticize the woman who aborts because the child she is carrying presents an inconvenience or because it is the 'wrong' sex, for example. But, were she or any other woman who had aborted to come to me to talk, I would try my best—knowing that I am not trained for pastoral activities—to listen. But this is not the same as not to criticize, depending upon the particulars. By pro-life moderate I simply mean that I understand that abortion can never be eliminated entirely—that is utopian—and, moreover, I do not believe the way to do politics around this issue is to call for constitutional amendment or criminal legislation. That seems to me a mistake that does not reflect the views of the vast majority of Americans and is not required by a moral commitment against abortion-on-demand. The majority of Americans do not believe that all, or perhaps even most, abortions should be criminalized, but they believe that abortion can and should be restricted and rare, seen for the serious matter that it is."

"I see, wishy-washy is another way to put it. Middle-of-the-road and all that. That doesn't seem to be resoundingly ethical and you are officially a professor of ethics. Why don't you just bite the bullet: yes or no, pro or con?"

"There is a big difference between wishy-washing and principled moderation. My position recognizes both the moral complexity of the issue and the complexities of what it means to do politics around this issue in our pluralistic society. Nearly fifteen years ago I wrote: 'I cannot accept an absolute prohibition on abortion. But I do not—and cannot—see that 'right' as absolute. . . . For I am in fact part of a large majority that opposes both abortion on demand and an absolute restriction on abortion.' This position hasn't gained much of a hearing. Mind you, I'm not arguing that majoritarianism should govern morality. If polls had been taken in 1860 showing that the vast majority of Americans, northern and southern, favored slavery, I would have said then— at least, I pray to God I would have said then, that the vast majority is wrong and here's why. One cannot presume that the right thing to do is always the most popular. But Americans have shown both nuance and unsettlement in their views on abortion. Most of the pro-life people I know, anguished over abortion, are nonetheless prepared to move slowly to build in certain restraints. The most intransigent interlocutors I encounter in the world of the academic at conferences and the like are the pro-choice absolutists."

"Aha! I knew it. Covertly your real position is coming out. You are just anti-choice. Admit it."

"Consider your language. 'Anti-choice,' you say, knowing that makes a person un-American straight off, doesn't it, for we have made 'choice' the trump card in any argument. If someone chooses, it is right, or at least unassailable. No one can argue. Are you sure you want to commit yourself to this? Are you sure you want to place yourself in a position where you can never criticize the 'choices' or so-called choices people make? Let me recount for you an unforgettable moment from one of my classes, one I taught for years some years ago now, called 'Feminist Politics and Theory.' Abortion was on the table for discussion. Many pleasant young women—all white, and that is critical to the tale—were intoning the by-then laid-down official line on pro-choice, which always includes the kicker: 'But even if I have some doubts about it, poor people, especially blacks, need abortion and they are powerless and can't argue for it so it's up to us to make the case.' A young black woman in the class, her hands actually trembling from anger, called back: 'Don't tell me that you are doing me a big favor by saying I can abort my babies because it's my right and somehow this will make my situation better. It won't.' She's right. It hasn't made it better. The years since 1973—years dominated by a notion that the ethic of 'choice' is the end-all and be-all of moral and political argumentation—have seen a tremendous advance, of a professional, socioeconomic sort, for relatively well-placed, white upper-middle-class professionals. But what else have we seen? A general coarsening of life. An explosion of smut and misogyny. The tremendous upsurge in our midst of a predatory ethic which dictates by definition that the most defenseless suffer the most. A tremendous increase in child abuse and abandonment. That was supposed to disappear when every child was 'wanted,' or don't you remember the sunny publicity to this effect? As well, we have seen an upsurge in out-of-wedlock teen pregnancies, a dismal statistic in which the United States is now the world's leader. And, because of that, the United States is also high in its rate of infant mortality. Without asserting any strict causal connections here, do you really think this is all disconnected? Perhaps you ought to consider that the vast majority of pro-life activists are women, not men. Why are they doing that? What are the concerns of the women involved? Should these issues have no weight whatsoever? Perhaps women who embrace what they see as a consistent 'ethic of life' understand a few things. Perhaps we destroy whatever stands in our way through language first—even the language of law—and a general diminution of social respect and human decency follows."

"This seems hyperbolic and flawed to me. Surely you are not saying that *Roe v. Wade* somehow caused all these other problems. Give me a break! That is just plain unfair and faulty logic as well."

"No, I wasn't making a causal argument, remember. I was making a contextual one. Let me try to flesh this out because, obviously, I have not been clear. As George McKenna argued in a landmark piece in the *Atlantic Monthly*, 'On Abortion: A Lincolnian Position,' we do well to remember that abortion now is 'one of the most carefully cultivated institutions in America.' This is important. The key is *institutions*. Abortion is much more than a matter of individuals lining up and choosing. 'It is protected by courts, subsidized by legislatures, performed in government-run hospitals and clinics, and promoted as a "fundamental right" by our State Department.' The official power is on that side, not with the pro-life forces. Indeed, the full weight of federal power has been placed on the abortion side, especially under the current administration. The 1993 health-care bill, had it passed, 'would have nationalized the funding of abortion, compelling everyone to buy a "standard package" that included it.' Yet those who favor the current abortion regime continue to act as if theirs is the beleagured side, as if they are the ones under pressure. This is ludicrous. When the United States Supreme Court, in a situation of volatile and deep moral division, throws *all* its weight to one side of a divide, the moral and civic universe has been riven in a particular way. It is no wonder the politics surrounding abortion is so harsh and often so desperate. How do you fight this concatenation of official governmental and legal and medical power? How do you struggle against the depletion of the possibilities for serious engagement around the question when our language has become diminished through the abstracted euphemisms the 'pro-choice' forces embrace? I began to worry about this years ago, thinking of George Orwell's great essay on 'Politics and the English Language,' with its reminder of the many ways the powerful have comforted themselves even as they were ravaging and pillaging by speaking of such matters as 'rural relocation' rather than harrying the countryside, destroying the peasants, and displacing whole peoples. We, too, are guilty of mangling plain language in order to avoid the concrete reality of human life-in-process. And when that happens it becomes almost impossible to do politics.

Just to gain a minimal hearing, the aggrieved side—in this case, pro-life—often has to up the rhetorical ante. And then the other side says, 'Look, see what we told you! These people are extremists!' Remember: a politics was going on around abortion before *Roe v. Wade.* Citizens were slogging it out. Many legislative options were on the table. In 1973 about 60 percent of the nation's population lived within 100 miles—a two-hour drive—of a state with a legalized abortion law. And, as historian Michael Barone points out, 'just as the Supreme Court was speaking, legislatures in almost all of the states were going into session; many would probably have liberalized their abortion laws if the court had not acted.' So what we had in *Roe* was a disruption of citizen politics and the juridicalization and medicalization of the issue. Those opposed were cut out of the debate, their concerns rendered illegitimate. Now, remember, that concern is about who is or is not within the boundary of the moral community. It is not about excluding people; it is about including them."

"Here we go. Inclusion. Compassion. I can see it coming. You are perilously close to portraying all pro-choice people as pro-choice absolutists, hence, villains. Aren't you engaged in a little bit of polemicizing and silencing of your own here?"

"I hope not. I'm just trying to point out that folks who are backed up against the wall often respond in ardent ways. But I am not calling for immoderation. I am calling for reason and judgment—for practical reason of the sort Aristotle insisted was what political argumentation was all about. I understand full well that not every political issue can or must be doctrinalized in line with a set of theological commitments. As well, not every doctrinal issue should be politicized. I oppose alliances of throne and altar. But that isn't the issue. The Catholic Church, for example, is clear that its position on contraception, derived from natural law, is binding on Catholics only. Abortion is another matter. That involves the entire community. The issue is depletion of the moral universe and the collapse of any decent consideration for those we have first excised and dehumanized through language. That's one issue. Another is the way in which proponents of the current abortion regime constantly label their opponents as religious fanatics even as they press for the cleansing of political argumentation from religious commitments in a way that would have silenced Abraham Lincoln, silenced Sojourner Truth, silenced Martin Luther King, silenced Dorothy Day, silenced Jane Addams. Who is extreme here?"

"I'm unconvinced. You seem to be making a lot out of rhetoric. Words. Words. Words. Words are ephemeral things. I don't understand this preoccupation. You seem to put too much weight by far on mere rhetoric."

"Mere rhetoric is always what we call it when we don't want to consider the implications of the words we use. Should we not be wary of language that throws up a linguistic barrier between the individual and the reality and conflict of abortion? Christopher Hitchens, himself both atheist and Marxist, observed this when, writing in *The Nation*, he reminded the readers of that very left-wing publication that abortion involves something *real*. He wrote: 'But anyone who has ever seen a sonogram or has spent even an hour with a textbook on embryology knows that emotions are not the deciding factor. In order to terminate a pregnancy, you have to still a heartbeat, switch off a developing brain, and, whatever the method, break some bones and rupture some organs.' He sympathizes, he says, with the 'genuine, impressive, unforced revulsion at the idea of a disposable fetus.' Walker Percy, years earlier, in a brilliant cri de coeur, proclaimed, in effect, pile on obfuscation after obfuscation and the material reality remains— 'it lives.' Here, for example, is some morally distancing language that places the unborn entirely outside the purview of ethical consideration: descriptions of the fetus as a parasite, a tenant, an airborne spore, or, God help us, property. Commented political theorist, Philip Abbott, about such examples: 'The world of the philosopher is filled with people seeds, child missile launchers, Martians, talking robots, jigsaw cells that form human beings, transparent wombs—everything in fact but fetuses growing in wombs and infants cradled in parents' arms.' And the reaction of the philosophers Abbott has in his sights to such an argument? This revulsion, according to Michael Tooley, is exactly like the 'reaction of previous generations to masturbation or oral sex.' It is an atavistic hangover from an earlier era. Tooley's own position even permits unrestricted infanticide. Whether a child should live or die is the parents' choice, especially likely to be exercised where the imperfect unborn or even born are concerned. They are prime candidates for elimination—after we have first dehumanized them through language. We live in an era when a new eugenics is coming at us like a runaway freight train. This being the case, it is ever more likely that, in the name of compassion and of improving the species, less than perfect human beings will be eliminated in large numbers. Of course, compassion will be stressed. Children with retardation will suffer so they should be 'allowed to die' or, preferably, be surgically expelled before birth. Persons with physical handicaps suffer; it follows that it would be better were they not born. Wrongful life, we call it."

"Doesn't this just invite compulsion? Aren't you moving into coercion—forcing things down people's throats, including handicapped infants they may not want and be unable to care for?"

"Now you have hit on a key question. My worry is this: the more we insist that we can intervene in the natural lottery and control whether a child is born black or white, gay or straight, male or female, 'normal' or 'abnormal,' the more we undercut the project of human compassion and political equality. For these are projects and accomplishments that help us to unlock our hearts before other human beings, that help us to say, 'There but for the grace of God,' that call us to a generous notion of the human community and that demand real practical efforts, not just comforting words. We have a regime of so-called reproductive freedom. And we devote less all the time to children. We need more support for mothers, fathers, and families. More attention to those who do not abort. It is unfair to claim that pro-life advocates care only about fetuses, not living children and women. Last year the archdiocese of New York, strapped to the bone by its soup kitchens, its AIDS-care centers, its elderly outreach, and its homeless shelters, devoted $5 million to help 50,000 women in situations of unintended pregnancies, writes Todd David Whitmore in an essay in *The Christian Century*, adding that 'this is a remark-

able effort unmatched by any other intermediary institution.'
And it is happening in archdiocesan centers around the country.
Why do we know so little of this? In the meantime, the National
Abortion Rights Action League garners millions every years for
its 'war chest' to fight even the most minimal restrictions on abortion on demand, including third trimester and partial birth abortions. They do not devote one penny to help pregnant women
who 'choose' to carry their babies to term. But let me return to
the contextual argument I was making, not so much, then, a matter of laying down the law as of 'thinking what we are doing,' in
the words of Hannah Arendt. Should a politics of technological control and an ethos of unadorned consequentialism grow
apace, as I fear it will, what will be the likely result for families and
for the wider society? Minimally, I see an erosion of the bases of
trust, including an ethic of stewardship and care, an ethic that
respects the richness, the diversity, the intrinsic value of forms of
life and that sees a person as a friend and as one's neighbor, not
primarily as a chooser or aggrandizer. When we concurred, as a
society, to a nearly full-scale redefinition of life that placed developing human life *altogether* outside the boundary of moral consideration, I believe we suffered a deep, if subtle, moral corruption.
I think of others once hidden from view so that we were not required to see them. In acting unthinkingly, we simply acquiesce in
the dominant terms of the hard-edged discourse of our day: looking out for number one, life as a zero-sum game, you have your
opinion, I have mine. If we continue down this path, we may one
day tip the balance toward a society whose reigning symbol is ex-
pendability, elimination of whatever is inconvenient, whatever
gets in the way."

"This seems to me just so much sermonizing. Remember, we
are talking about choice here—about individual choice."

"But there are all sorts of ways we restrict choice. We don't let
people own slaves. We don't let people kill their living children
because they get in the way. We don't let people choose to smoke
in nearly all public places. You can't choose to knock over a person in a wheelchair because she is in your fast-moving way. You

can't choose to torture a dog. You can't choose to put dangerous drugs into your own body. Or, if you make these choices, there is a price to pay. Every society places restraints on individual freedom. Why no possibility of *any* restraint on abortion? When Pennsylvania moved to end abortion for reasons of sex selection, the leaders of NARAL set up a clamor about coercion and restriction of choice. But no right is unlimited. What, then, is going on here? Can't we see a common, good issue lurking in the interstices of this issue? Why should female embryos—the most likely to be aborted for sex-preference reasons—be considered a defect worthy of elimination? In other places on our globe, throw-away children, most of them girls, end up dying in crowded orphanages— their gender isn't wanted. Surely we should challenge differential treatment based on sex from the beginning to the end of life. It's an odd feminism that doesn't take account of this issue."

"Well, it seems to me that you take account of just about everything except the pregnant woman herself. Why doesn't she figure in the overall structure of your argument? Don't you appreciate how desperate a woman can be? Have you no sympathy at all with her plight?"

"In fact, I am trying to take account of the complexity and pathos of situations in which a woman feels desperate or has been abandoned or is at the end of her tether. Do we help her by continuing to push the rhetoric of choice? That doesn't build in a sustaining community. That doesn't afford any real comfort save the cold comfort of abortion. I believe we have been callous about women's feelings in this matter. Women are supposed to go for it, have the 'procedure,' and have done with it. To be sure, a woman may feel relieved, especially if she has no one supporting her in her situation. But the stalwart exerciser of a basic right? I don't think so. It is far more complicated, far more solemn, far more filled with foreboding thoughts. Yet if the woman feels badly, it gets treated, at least in much feminist argumentation, as so much 'false-consciousness.' "

"It seems to me that, deep down, you want to end all abortions, then. Why don't you just say that?"

"Because it is not so simple. In a perfect world, there would be no abortions and no murders and no abused children and no wars and all the rest. But we live in a very imperfect world where all those things exist and always will. Albert Camus, in the aftermath of the horror that was the Second World War, cried out that, although we cannot create a world in which no child suffers, we can do our best to reduce the incidence of suffering. I say this: no decent person believes that abortion is a positive moral good. So let us move to discourage and to restrain; to roll back the tide a bit; to unlock our hearts once again to a more complex set of moral claims and arguments. I am not interested in imposing my 'subjective viewpoint' on everybody else. This is a common-good issue. It has to do with something real and palpable: Who is in and who is out of that moral community we call America? It is a civic matter, a concern for all citizens. It is time for our moral squeamishness to come to the surface rather than being quashed, perhaps because we fear giving offense or being very un-p.c. But remember this: the developing human is human. The burden of proof should always be on those who propose to take a life, even in situ. That is the way our jurisprudence usually works. That is the way we forestall arbitrary or reckless disregard for human life. The burden should be on those who propose to 'still heartbeats and crush bones.' Currently, we are in the moral twilight zone. Consider that we charge a person with double homicide if he kills a pregnant woman; for double manslaughter if a pregnant woman dies in an automobile accident caused by a drunk driver. Physicians operate on the unborn as full-fledged patients, patients that might, on some other operating table, be candidates only for killing. The least we can do, as a beginning point, is to acknowledge the *human* status of what we propose to eliminate. And to go from there into the difficult, sometimes terrible necessities—those exceedingly rare moments when it really is the mother's life poised against the baby's. The politics around this issue will be with us for a long time to come. The moral questions have always been there. That we have chosen to ignore them—for *Roe* gave us permission to do precisely that—doesn't mean anything was resolved. President

Vaclav Havel of the Czech Republic has excoriated what he calls the 'arrogant anthropocentrism of modern man who believes that he can control everything; that he is the master of all he surveys; that he can order life and death as he sees fit' as lying at the basis of our current crisis. He is right. Abortion, seen in this light, becomes a technological resolution to what is construed as a woman's 'control deficit' in the overall scheme of life given the particularities of her embodiment. But the problem here is the view of life that secretes such an evaluation of woman's embodiment, surely!"

The dialogue, for now, is over for the purpose of these reflections. But let us imagine the world we hope our children will know. A world that is more kind than cruel. A world that is sturdy, safe, and decent. That is not the world many of our children find, and some will not have the chance to experience the world at all. As we near the end of this harsh century, we Americans should not be touting our triumphs so much as examining our consciences by asking ourselves whether we remain what Lincoln hoped we would always be—the last best hope on earth. You be the judge.

Notes

1. Whether this case was decided on the best possible grounds is a separate matter. That the days of de jure segregation had to end seems to me beyond dispute.

2. For a helpful summary of *Roe* and subsequent decisions and controversies surrounding it see Ian Shapiro, ed., *Abortion: The Supreme Court Decisions* (Indianapolis: Hackett, 1995).

3. Of course, the whole "penumbra" business is another instance regarded by many constitutional law thinkers as a dubious piece of ingenious extra-constitutional reasoning.

4. Subsequent decisions, until recently, bolstered *Roe*. *Planned Parenthood v. Danforth* in 1976 denied the husband any role in the abortion decision and removed parents of unwed minors from the circle of concern. *Colautti v. Franklin* in 1979 affirmed that the physician's discretionary power to determine viability was pretty much absolute. Three deci-

sions in 1983 etched ever deeper in stone limits to any power of the states to regulate. This began to shift slightly by 1990 with the *Webster* case.

5. See the discussion in Shapiro, ed., *Abortion*, and in Elizabeth Mensch and Alan Freeman, *The Politics of Virtue* (Durham, N.C.: Duke University Press, 1993), 128.

CHAPTER TEN

Judicial Power and Abortion Politics:
Roe v. Wade

GEORGE WILL

Jean Elshtain, like many people who think clearly and write carefully about political things, knows her Orwell, and particularly his essay on "Politics and the English Language," wherein he says that insincerity is an enemy of clarity. That insight came to mind when Kate Michelman of the National Abortion and Reproduction Rights Action League spoke against banning the procedure commonly called partial birth abortion. In that procedure the baby is four-fifths delivered—all but a portion of the skull, which is collapsed when the brains are sucked out. Michelman argued that procedure is not as inhuman as it might seem because the baby is dead before the skull is collapsed; he or she is killed early in the procedure by the anesthesia given to the mother.

Michelman's assertion was, in fact, false, but that is not what made it fascinating. Rather, its significance was in the language she used. She did not say that the anesthetic kills the baby. Rather, she said that because of the anesthetic, the baby "undergoes demise." What an odd and telling locution. It tells us that Michelman is uneasy. Surely when she puts herbicide on her lawn, she does not say that her crabgrass "undergoes demise." Surely she says that she kills her crabgrass.

Now, the awkward unclarity of Michelman's locution is a form of flinching from the stark, cold fact that the Supreme Court put at the center of national politics in 1973. Abortion kills. It deliberately terminates not merely a "pregnancy" but a new human being in the intrauterine (embryonic or fetal) stage of its development. How we should think and feel about the life taken by abortion is a matter about which thoughtful people can honorably disagree.

But a few things are indisputable, even though the Court in *Roe v. Wade* bungled them badly. The Court declared that a fetus is "potential life." No: a fetus is alive and biologically human. As Walker Percy, an M.D. as well as a novelist, wrote, it is a commonplace of modern biology that a life "begins when the chromosomes of the sperm fuse with the chromosomes of the ovum to form a new DNA complex that thenceforth directs the ontogenesis of the organism." As Percy said, "The onset of individual life is not a dogma of the church but a fact of science. How much more convenient if we lived in the thirteenth century, when no one knew anything about microbiology and arguments about the onset of life were legitimate."

So, the Supreme Court illegitimately proclaimed an inability to say when life begins. Illegitimately, but conveniently, because science defeats the project of presenting abortion as akin to removing a tumor, or a hamburger, from the woman's stomach. Biology does not allow the abortion argument to be about, or for anyone to be agnostic about, when human life begins. The argument, in which thoughtful and decent people differ, is about the moral significance and proper legal status of fetal life, which sometimes conflicts with other values, at various stages of the gestational continuum.

For twenty-five years we have been, and for many more than twenty-five years we will be, living with the lingering aftershocks of what the Court did when it decided to short-circuit democracy, truncating legislative debates and constitutionalizing the abortion controversy. When, with the scythe of *Roe v. Wade*, the Court mowed down the abortion laws of all fifty states, those laws were in flux. In the five years immediately before 1973, eighteen states with 41 percent of the population had liberalized their abortion laws. By 1973, two-thirds of Americans lived in those fourteen states or within a 100-mile drive of one of them. "Abortion rights" in some form—actually, in various forms, thanks to federalism—were part of American political life; Americans were reasoning through the tangle of their conflicting thoughts about the subject.

In the process of bringing that deliberation to an abrupt halt, *Roe v. Wade* littered the landscape with confusions. Finding constitutional significance in the fact that the number nine is divisible by three, the Court decreed that the status of the fetus changes with the trimesters of pregnancy, although the trimesters are both medically and morally meaningless. The Court then disregarded plain biology and adopted a stance of being too modest to say when life begins. But the Court then turned around and immodestly answered a deep philosophic mystery by decreeing when "meaningful" life begins. It defined viability as the point at which "meaningful" life can be lived outside the womb. Thus, was constitutional law linked to a dynamic science that could move viability earlier into gestation?

The Court in *Roe* asserted it to be a fact that fetuses are not "persons in the whole sense" and do not possess constitutional rights. But from that supposed fact it does not follow that the state cannot prevent the killing of them. As John Hart Ely has observed, dogs are not "persons in the whole sense" and do not possess constitutional rights, but can be to some extent protected from killing. So, twenty-five years after *Roe v. Wade*, consider some of the following consequences of failure to think carefully about this.

During the Senate debate about banning partial birth abortions, Pennsylvania's Rick Santorum, an advocate of the ban, asked two opponents of the ban, Wisconsin's Russ Feingold and New Jersey's Frank Lautenberg, to suppose something. Suppose, Santorum said, that during a partial birth abortion procedure a baby, instead of being only four-fifths delivered, slips all the way out of the mother. Santorum asked if the two senators thought that killing the born baby would still be a "choice" the mother had a constitutionally protected right to make. Feingold said yes, it would be up to the woman and her doctor. Lautenberg agreed.

We have a record of this exchange only because C-SPAN covered it. The Congressional Record, ostensibly the record of what is said on the Senate floor, does not read the way the debate actually unfolded. The two senators subsequently altered—falsified—the record. By the way, this exchange occurred two months after the nation's attention was riveted by two college students being charged with murder for doing essentially what the two senators said was a constitutional right: they killed the son they did not want, minutes after he had been born in a Delaware motel room.

In 1982 Pennsylvania passed a law requiring that a woman seeking an abortion be informed of possible detrimental physical and psychological effects of abortion; the probable gestational age of her fetus and the anatomical and physical characteristics of fetuses at two-week gestational increments; alternatives to abortion; available assistance for prenatal, childbirth, and neonatal expenses; and the fact that fathers must assist child support. In 1986 the Supreme Court ruled, 5–4, that this law was an unconstitutional violation of a woman's privacy right because the law was— listen carefully to this—an "intrusive informational prescription." The privacy right had become a right not to be informed.

In various jurisdictions, courts have, in effect, taken custody of fetuses. In Baltimore, a pregnant drug abuser was placed under court jurisdiction to prevent her from jeopardizing the health of her fetus. Of course she retained the fundamental privacy right to kill the fetus with an abortion.

Prenatal medicine's expanding arsenal of diagnostic and therapeutic techniques now makes possible intrauterine treatment of many forms of fetal distress and genetic problems. Drugs and blood transfusions can be administered to fetuses, and excess fluids can be drained from their skulls and lungs. So mothers have a constitutional privacy right to kill, at any time, fetuses that doctors, bound by their Hippocratic oath to "do no harm," can and do treat as patients.

Enough. These anecdotes reveal where we are. How can we get to higher, less swampy ground?

Law can compel cultural changes, and regarding abortion it has done that. But law also must follow the culture, and the stark cultural fact is that abortion, which ends one-quarter of American pregnancies, is now a more common surgical procedure than circumcision. Suppose *Roe v. Wade* were overturned, either by the Court reversing itself or by a minimalist constitutional amendment that simply stated that nothing in the Constitution shall be construed as establishing a right to abortion. What then would

195

happen in today's America? There probably is not a state in the Union—not Utah, not Louisiana—that would ban abortion in the first trimester. Such abortions today are the overwhelming majority of all abortions.

However, were abortion restored to its status prior to 1973—to a matter subject to regulation by the states—the public could and would envelop the practice of abortion in laws expressing the nuances and ambivalence in the public's thinking about abortion. These laws would range from mandates for parental notification when abortions are sought by minors, to prohibitions (with narrow exceptions) on late-term abortions.

The country might increasingly come to fit Jean Elshtain's' description of herself as a "pro-life moderate." After all, this is a deeply conflicted country concerning this subject. Young couples who fancy themselves progressive and modern, and hence "pro-choice," are admirably eager, when blessed with pregnancy, to invest great energy in securing the best prenatal care, including sonograms. Today's sonograms can reveal the fingers and the chambers of the heart of an eighteen-week-old fetus. And sonograms produce pictures suitable for framing. Those pictures adorn the homes of parents who describe themselves as pro-choice even while they read a book very popular with young parents, *The Well Baby Book*, which says: "Increasing knowledge is increasing the awe and respect we have for the unborn baby and is causing us to regard the unborn baby as a real person long before birth."

Just so. But the Court will not allow a free evolution of the public's sensibilities through a process of democratic persuasion. That is why, at bottom, the scandal of *Roe v. Wade* is less that the Court made a hash of the questions it tried to answer, but that it undertook to answer a policy question that the Constitution does not make the business of the Court.

Now, what about the privacy right?

Leave aside whether or not it is helpful or obfuscating to say, as a justice famously said, that the privacy right is an emanation of a penumbra of other rights. Let us stipulate that some sorts of privacy implicate constitutional values. After all, the Constitution erects protections against unreasonable searches and seizures. And by protecting private property, the Constitution protects a liberal society's principal bulwark of privacy. That is, private property is a prerequisite for limited government and an open society because private property erects around the individual a zone of sovereignty.

But what does the privacy right mean regarding abortion? The privacy right was postulated without reference to abortion. As late as 1970 the reference was not to the right of people to choose whatever sexual lives they wanted. Rather, in the context of access to contraception, the Court identified the privacy right as a way of affirming and protecting the social institution of marriage. A few years later, in *Roe*, the Court took a radical turn away from, and actually against, its prior reasoning.

Concerning abortion, it presented the privacy right as an emanation, so to speak, of radical individualism. It said a woman's privacy right entailed a right to abortion because respect for individual autonomy entails such a right. Individual autonomy seemed suddenly to be a value that would trump all competing values.

But of course it cannot trump all others. The privacy right is not a right to live without interference from government. America may be increasingly anarchic, but America's public philosophy is not anarchism. And the privacy right is not a right to do whatever one wants with one's body. Were it such a right, we would owe a large apology, and perhaps a large sum of restitution, to drug dealers who have been serving jail sentences for the crime of serving the desires of some Americans to put cocaine and heroin into their bodies.

Let me be clear. The Court has a great and stately jurisdiction, construing a Constitution written to protect society from significant ills and evils, as the founders envisioned them, and the Court is supposed to wield the Constitution against the twentieth-century counterparts of those ills and evils. But, really: Are regulation of abortion, and protection of fetal life, such ills and evils?

Unfortunately, the Court, far from being chastened by the results of its antidemocratic arrogance, has become steadily more impatient and cranky about the fact that the public will not shut up and leave the justices to their chosen (albeit unassigned) work of writing social policy. In 1992, on the morning when the Court was about to hand down its ruling in *Planned Parenthood v. Casey*, a case that could have been, but did not turn out to be, an occasion for overturning *Roe v. Wade*, Justice Kennedy, reveling in his role as a swing vote in a closely divided Court, invited into his chambers a journalist to record his own self-dramatization. Kennedy stood at the window of his chamber, looking down at the crowds waiting outside for the Court's decision, and he said to the journalist, "Sometimes you don't know if you're Caesar about to cross the Rubicon or Captain Queeg cutting your own tow line." Good grief.

As Mary Ann Glendon has written, the Court's opinion that day, read and presumably written (at least in part) by Kennedy, did indeed have a "Caesarian—or at least an imperious—ring." It told the American people, in effect, to shape up, pipe down, and fall in line. It said the Court has the authority to "speak before all others" concerning American "constitutional ideals." And it said that Americans would be "tested"—Kennedy's word—by their willingness to toe the line the Court lays down concerning those ideals. And, most annoyingly, Kennedy called on "the contending sides of a national controversy to end their national division by accepting a common mandate rooted in the Constitution." In other words, we the judiciary say to we the people, "Shut up, we declare this debate over."

Here is some bad news for Kennedy and others who have created intellectual chaos and political turmoil by nationalizing the abortion controversy, and doing so by manufacturing a spurious constitutional imperative that seems to make dissent an impiety toward the Constitution. The news is that, paradoxically, the Court's attempt to shove aside the process of democratic persuasion has instead energized the country's largest current grass-roots movement—the right-to-life movement, a genuine insurgency.

As Elshtain says, the pro-choice movement likes to present itself as an embattled insurgency, but it actually is the establishment. Abortion, particularly under the current national administration is, as George McKenna has written in the *Atlantic Monthly*, one of America's "most carefully cultivated institutions." That is, "It is protected by courts, subsidized by legislatures, performed in government-run hospitals and clinics, and promoted abroad as a 'fundamental right' by our State Department." Indeed, even Planned Parenthood is a semi-subsidiary of the federal government, receiving one-third of its budget therefrom.

But abortion in its current status and prevalence is not more firmly entrenched than another "peculiar institution" was when the Supreme Court said, in the matter of Dred Scott, that the country should simmer down and let the Court settle things. The institution of slavery had just eight more years to live.

Now, I am not suggesting that abortion can or should be abolished. Rather, I am saying that this is not the sort of controversy in which courts can or should have the final say. The only way they can do that is by giving the issue an artificial and unconvincing clarity—trimesters, "viability," "meaningful life," and all the rest. Furthermore, courts tend to take such controversies out of the realm of negotiable differences by casting them in what Mary Ann Glendon characterizes as the hard-edged, absolutist language of individual rights, excluding considerations of community interests and values that would be weighed in a properly balanced legislative setting for making policy.

Such exclusion has consequences. Consider this. The quarter of a century since *Roe v. Wade* has seen a sudden, unanticipated social earthquake of tragic proportions—the explosive increase of births out of wedlock. *Roe v. Wade* severely defined abortion—the ending of pregnancy—as the sole prerogative of a woman. Is it not possible that this subtly, even subliminally, encouraged the notion that pregnancy is solely a woman's problem? She stands there autonomous. But perhaps also isolated and lonely.

Abortion policy as the Court began manufacturing it in *Roe v. Wade* reflects what Michael Sandel has identified as the ideal of the "unencumbered self." But what are considered burdensome encumbrances may actually be community values and attachments that make life commodious for social creatures such as we. We are in deep and turbulent philosophic waters here, and it is—fortunately—beyond the powers of the Court to order an end of the argument that it has so improvidently made its own.

NEW FORUM BOOKS

New Forum Books makes available to general readers outstanding original inter-disciplinary scholarship with a special focus on the juncture of culture, law, and politics. New Forum Books is guided by the conviction that law and politics not only reflect culture, but help to shape it. Authors include leading political scientists, sociologists, legal scholars, philosophers, theologians, historians, and economists writing for nonspecialist readers and scholars across a range of fields. Looking at questions such as political equality, the concept of rights, the problem of virtue in liberal politics, crime and punishment, population, poverty, economic development, and the international legal and political order, New Forum Books seeks to explain—not explain away—the difficult issues we face today.

Paul Edward Gottfried, *After Liberalism: Mass Democracy in the Managerial State*

Peter Berkowitz, *Virtue and the Making of Modern Liberalism*

John E. Coons and Patrick M. Brennan, *By Nature Equal: The Anatomy of a Western Insight*

David Novak, *Covenantal Rights: A Study in Jewish Political Theory*

Charles L. Glenn, *The Ambiguous Embrace: Government and Faith-Based Schools and Social Agencies*

Peter Bauer, *From Subsistence to Exchange and Other Essays*

Robert P. George, ed., *Great Cases in Constitutional Law*